MANUAL ON GENDER MAINSTREAMING
AT UNIVERSITIES

This project is realised with the support of the European Commission
This report reflects the authors' view. The Commission is not liable for any use
that may be made of the information contained here.

Authors:
Ils Stevens & Ilse Van Lamoen

KATHOLIEKE
UNIVERSITEIT
LEUVEN

Centrum
voor
Gender en Diversiteit

UNIVERSITEIT
MAASTRICHT

Manual on Gender Mainstreaming at Universities

'Equal Opportunities at Universities.
Towards a Gender Mainstreaming Approach'

June 2001

Leuven-Apeldoorn

Manual on Gender Mainstreaming at Universities
'Equal Opportunities at Universities.
Towards a Gender Mainstreaming Approach'
Leuven – Apeldoorn
Garant
2001

164 blz. – 24 cm
D/2001/5779/114
ISBN 90-441-1196-5
NUGI: 665/729

Omslagontwerp: Danni Elskens

Garant
Tiensesteenweg 91, 3010 Leuven – Kessel-Lo (België)
Koninginnelaan 96, 7315 EB Apeldoorn (Nederland)
uitgeverij@garant.be

CONTENT

Chapter 2:
Gender mainstreaming at universities: the instrumental approach   39

Chapter 3:
Gender Mainstreaming at universities: the process model approach

PREFACE

In 2000 the concern of the European Commission about the under-representation of women in the different fields of science, technology and development led to the publication of the ETAN-report "Promoting excellence through mainstreaming gender equality". The report was commissioned by the European Commission's Research Directorate-General and prepared by the European Technology Assessment Network (ETAN) expert working group on women in science. It stated: *"In the interests of social justice and the need to foster excellence in scientific endeavour in the European Union, we invite stakeholders to respond to our recommendations not only with words, but also by taking appropriate actions to correct the gender imbalance in science."*

To achieve a better gender balance in universities, research institutes and knowledge-organisations a consortium of institutions involved in gender mainstreaming set up the research project "Equal opportunities at Universities. Towards a gender mainstreaming approach" (Project VS/2000/0358-DG EMPL/D/5-SI2.244161). The main aim of the project was to exchange information and experiences concerning equal opportunities policies and gender mainstreaming in the context of universities and research institutes, in order to develop a manual on the mainstreaming strategy, tailor made for universities. The project was to cover one year, but was reduced to nine months for technical reasons. As a consequence of this reduction in combination with the fact that providing practical guidance of the mainstreaming process in universities is breaking new grounds, not all paragraphs in the manual are elaborated in detail. The choice was made to develop a general framework for mainstreaming at universities making use of the newest insights and presenting a selection of examples and good practices.

The target group of the manual are all organisations that employ scientists in the broadest sense, going from people in engineering and technology to academics in the social sciences and the humanities. It particularly addresses academic leaders, managers and policy makers with specific responsibilities in universities and research institutions or working in the variety of faculties, departments and service units, at central and at decentralised levels. The manual is also very useful for scientists themselves, women and men.

The research was carried out by Ils Stevens (Katholieke Universiteit Leuven/K.U.Leuven) and Drs. Ilse Van Lamoen (Universiteit Maastricht/ U.M.), who were in the first phase assisted by Chantal Caes (UM). The project was designed and co-ordinated by Elsy Van Roy (K.U.Leuven) and was supervised by Prof. Dr. Bea Van Buggenhout (K.U.Leuven) and Dr. Mineke Bosch (UM). The administrative support was taken care of by Brigitte Corthouts and Katrien Caron (K.U.Leuven)

The partners in the consortium were:

Co-ordinator: Centre for Equal Opportunities Policies, Katholieke Universiteit Leuven, Belgium (Prof. Dr. Bea Van Buggenhout and Prof. Dr. Katlijn Malfliet).

Co-operating Partnership: Centre for Gender and Diversity, Universiteit Maastricht, The Netherlands (Dr. Mineke Bosch and Prof. Dr. Maaike Meijer).

Transnational Partners: Equal Opportunities Officer, University of Bonn, Germany (Dr. Ursula Maettig), School of Social Sciences, University of Cardiff, United Kingdom (Prof. Dr. Teresa Rees), National Institute for Population Research, Rome, Italy, (Dr. Rossella Palomba).

National Partners (Belgium): Amazone VZW (Ariane Dierckx), Université Catholique de Louvain, Groupe Interfacultaire Etudes Femmes (Prof. Dr. Ada Garcia and Marie-Noëlle Lambert), City of Leuven, Welfare Service (Kristel Wildiers), Province of Vlaams-Brabant, Service for Equal Opportunities (Jessy Clynen) and the Federal Ministry of Labour and Employment, Direction Equal Opportunities (Carla Rijmenams and Sophie Matkava).

The manual has to be considered as a first attempt to elaborate a coherent set of guidelines, tools, instruments and good practices to support specific actions to realise gender mainstreaming at universities. Further efforts will be necessary to complete and refine the guidelines and tools, to test and adjust them through day-to-day practices and to adapt them to the specific context of knowledge-organisations in the different Member States.

It is a stepping stone on a long way forward!

ACKNOWLEDGEMENTS

We would like to thank our *transnational and national partners* for partici-pating so actively in the project, for reading the text over and over again, for reviewing and correcting it and for providing fresh ideas, references, illustrations and publications. We would also like to thank all partners for their active participation at the Expert Meetings organised in Belgium on 5-6 December 2000 and 24-25 April 2001.

Special thanks to *Dr. Sabine Hübner*, University of Bonn and *Dr. Alison Parken*, School of Social Sciences, University of Cardiff, who joined us at our second Partners Expert Meeting on 24-25 April 2001 and who since then have given such excellent input and support.

We would like to thank the Network of Mainstreaming Promoters at the K.U.Leuven, for providing us with their experiences and a lot of good practices. We have also benefit from the discussions held with some of the academic leaders, managers and scientists at University Maastricht who helped us to frame the basic challenges of today's universities. We thank *Drs. Anneke Eurelings, Prof. Dr. Hans Philipsen, Prof. Dr. Cor Spreeuwenberg, Prof. Dr. Paul Tummers and Dr. Liesbeth van Wely*.

Deserving a special mention are the people who reviewed the draft version of the manual. *Dr. Barbara Bagilhole*, Reader in Equal Opportu-nities in Social Policy, Department of Social Sciences, Loughborough University; *Dr. Diane Bebbington*, Research Officer for the Athena Project, Equality Challenge Unit for Higher Education, London; *Dr. Elizabeth Bird*, Department of Drama, Bristol University; *Dr. Barbara Hartung*, Niedersächsisches Ministerium für Wissenschaft und Kultur; *Dr. Andrea Löther & Dr. Brigitte Mühlenbruch*, Kompetenzzentrum Frauen in Wissenschaft und Forschung, University of Bonn; *Drs. Sarah Nelen*, Instituut voor de Overheid, K.U.Leuven; *Dr. Annelies van der Horst*, Project Manager Vrouwen Hogerop, Amsterdam.

A special thanking to *Prof. Dr. Teresa Rees* who – next to her appreciated partnership in the project – found the time to correct the English language, and to *Eamonn Forde* for going through the manual reviewing and correcting the English language of the newly written paragraphs and the last-minute changes.

A special mention also for *Brigitte Corthouts*, Secretary at the Centre for Equal Opportunities, K.U.Leuven who provided the administrative support for the project and took care of the correspondence of the partnerships, and for our webmaster *Dirk Maetens* who e-supported the project.

GENDER MAINSTREAMING: REACHING EXCELLENCE THROUGH CHANGE

Since gender mainstreaming was prompted onto the international policy agenda in 1995, the concept can hardly be thought about anymore as being removed from policy circles dealing with equal opportunity and diversity issues. This manual aims to facilitate the implementation of this innovative strategy in academic institutes. Its starting point is that gender mainstreaming is not just another burden to your already full agenda, but can become a key to your success. Mainstreaming gender equality – when applied well – is not an adverse strategy, but forms a vehicle to reach excellence through change. Its transforming potential makes it a valuable strategy for European academic institutes to maintain a leading role in today's knowledge society.

Most European universities were founded in a social context different from that of today. Whether their history goes back to the Middle Ages – when the first universities were founded – or whether they are relative newcomers in the field: all universities are confronted with similar changes. Developments like globalisation and Europeanisation, hybridisation of research, scaling-up and the attending need for competitiveness, affect the core activities of universities everywhere – their educational task, their research assignment and their social involvement.

All of these changes demand creative and energetic solutions. At the same time, the call for gender equality, as well as demands to make better use of women's potential in order to promote excellence, has become louder. The low percentage of female scientists, especially in the senior ranks, contrasts with the increasing gender balance in the academic student and graduate population. Are these challenges compatible?

In this manual we will argue that they are. In fact, gender mainstreaming enables you to get the best of two worlds. The manual's broad scope and its switching spotlights on the core activities of universities and the challenges they face in terms of management makes it interesting to anyone involved in academic policy making. No matter in which department or discipline you are working, if you are in any way involved in developing, adopting or executing policy – either as an academic leader, manager, policy maker or scientist – this manual will provide you with useful handles for thought and action. For you the challenge is to jump in and set yourself to mainstream!

The first chapter provides an introduction for anyone who wants to learn more about the merits of gender mainstreaming or wants to convince others of the need to promote it in their institute. After having set out the definition and basic principles of gender mainstreaming, we will illustrate, from various angles, that gender mainstreaming does not solely help you to cope with the challenges your university faces today but is actually a motor for promoting excellence in academic research, education and social involvement.

Once you are convinced that gender mainstreaming benefits your organisation, Chapter Two assists you in setting up a consistent policy strategy to implement gender mainstreaming all the way through your organisation. The tools and guidelines for gender mainstreaming as provided in this chapter are explicitly attuned to the academic context. They build on research results, experiences and good practices from various universities both in and outside Europe. The tools are structured in four categories: (i) measurement and monitoring; (ii) implementation and organisation; (ii) building awareness and ownership; and (iv) gender proofing and evaluation. Apart from an overview of instruments, the chapter provides practical recommendations on how to set priorities, utilize opportunities and prevent potential pitfalls.

In Chapter Three, the focus is shifted from a classical perspective on universities and their core activities in research, education and social involvement, to a management perspective on the quality and effectiveness of scientific organisations and their products and services. Based on the EFQM-model of excellence, a quality review model that proved its utility in the business and non-profit sector, the chapter challenges you to critically scrutinise customs and sacred cows in the production and organisation of science in your institute. By incorporating a gender perspective in all management areas as distinguished in the EFQM-model, we show you how gender mainstreaming can help you to enhance the enabling capacity of your institute and improve the quality of your products and services.

In principle, all chapters of this manual can be read separately. In relevant cases, we have included references for further explanation. The purposes of Chapter Two and Chapter Three basically are the same: both chapters show you how to implement gender mainstreaming in your organisation. But they start from a different angle. Chapter Two is structured around the categories of gender mainstreaming tools currently available. It explains how to apply them to your organisation as it exists today. Chapter Three starts with describing the challenges that universities are faced with in different management areas and shows you how gender mainstreaming can help you deal with those challenges. Depending on your personal interests or function in the organisation, you can step in wherever you want.

CHAPTER 1

WHAT IS GENDER MAINSTREAMING AND WHY IS IT A KEY TO SUCCESS?

When setting eyes on this manual or chancing upon the concept of gender mainstreaming for the first time your reaction might be coloured by a degree of reservation. Why would you take the trouble of implementing this new equal opportunities strategy if your university was already taking steps to promote women's participation in science? In this chapter we will argue that gender mainstreaming is more than a trendy policy phrase that wraps the age-old feminist demands in a new coating. The merits of gender mainstreaming range from increasing fairness and social justice to enlarging your organisation's attractiveness for both male and female scientists. Above all, gender mainstreaming stimulates you to critically review the production and organisation of science. Such a reflection is indispensable if you want to be able to respond adequately to the challenges your institute faces today. Gender mainstreaming urges you to uncover some of the myths surrounding scientific knowledge building, thereby clearing the way for a sane discussion on the quality, efficiency and social relevance of academic practices.

1.1 WHAT IS GENDER MAINSTREAMING?

Gender mainstreaming is an integral policy strategy for promoting equal opportunities that aims to mobilise all general policy programmes and practices to support the purposes of gender equality and diversity. The strategy does not restrict itself to specific measures to promote the advancement of women but pursues a situation in which all structures, values, and policy strategies in your institute are organised in such a way so that they equally serve the needs and interests of women and men. The ultimate aim is to establish a culture in which a diversity of people feel comfortable and respected, irrespective of sex, while individual talents have the room to develop in the directions that suit them best.

Gender mainstreaming is a proper strategy to address subtle forms of disadvantage or discrimination which nowadays are much more common than outright discrimination, something that, of course, has to be banned right away. Technically, women and men are each other's equals in today's academic world: women are free to enter the fields of research and education that interest them and the law forbids discrimination. But despite this formal equality, the academic arena is still characterised by numerous patterns of segregation between the sexes that can be largely traced to gender mechanisms.

Gender, as distinguished from sex, does not refer to the biological differences between women and men, but to the different roles and characteristics that are attributed to them in society. These roles and images are not fixed; rather they are historically and culturally determined. Most academic systems and structures as they exist today are based on models that were constructed centuries ago in a time in which universities were exclusively populated by men. They often reflect assumptions about the roles and tasks women and men have to perform in society that are seriously out of date and hinder a full use of human potential.

Gender mainstreaming, if applied well, helps you to ensure that your organisation does not maintain and strengthen traditional gender patterns in its own behaviour. To this end, all policy proposals, measures and procedures are critically reviewed, based on the question of whether or not they affect women and men differently, either directly or indirectly. As soon as (potential) gender biases are detected – either in access, judgements or outcomes – action is taken to adjust them in such a way that they contribute to gender equality. To guarantee that this is systematically done all the way through your organisation, all units and departments have the responsibility of integrating equal opportunities into all their regular actions and policy measures. Hence, the Council of Europe has formulated the following definition of gender mainstreaming: *"Gender mainstreaming is the (re)organisation, improvement, development and evaluation of policy processes so that a gender equality perspective is incorporated in all policies and at all stages by the actors normally involved in policy-making."*[1]

1.1.1 Where does gender mainstreaming come from?

Gender mainstreaming appeared for the first time in international texts after the United Nations Third World Conference on Women, which took place in Nairobi in 1985. Initially, the concept mainly concentrated on integrating women's roles and values in economic and social development programmes. As a precondition for governmental implementation, the United Nations were supposed to play a pioneering role in implementing the Nairobi *Forward Looking Strategies* in their ordinary work. All bodies of the UN were urged to set out a comprehensive policy on women's equality and incorporate it systematically into all their programmes, policy plans and strategic objectives.[2]

By carrying out the view that women's interests were not to be treated as side-aspects of regular policy programmes but that they had to be seen as an elementary part of them, the Nairobi conference gave an important impulse to the development of gender mainstreaming. The scope of the concept was extended and strengthened at the Fourth United Nations World Conference on Women (Beijing, 1995).[3] The *Platform for Action* that was adopted at this conference explicitly urged governments to "promote an active and visible policy of mainstreaming a gender perspective" in all critical areas of concern that were distinguished at the conference, including education and training.[4] By this explicit commitment to gender mainstreaming the Beijing *Platform for Action*, signed by 189 national governments, forcefully prompted the strategy on the international policy agenda.

In Europe, the institutes of the EU played a leading role in promoting gender mainstreaming as an auspicious strategy for establishing equal opportunities. In a Communication in 1996[5], the European Commission declared that the merits of gender mainstreaming are twofold: it can make equal opportunity actions far more efficient, while at the same time improving the quality of the policies which have been the subject of mainstreaming. In its *Fourth Medium Term Action Programme on Equal Opportunities* (1996-2000), the Commission formulated explicit policy lines to integrate equal opportunities into the preparation, implementation and monitoring of all EU and member state activities. Since then mainstreaming gender equality became a topic in various community policies and activities including the EU science policies.

1.1.2 EU policy initiatives to mainstream gender equality in science

When launching its *Fifth Framework Programme for Research and Technological Development* (1998-2002), the European Commission decided to include an equal opportunities dimension by promoting women's participation European research.[6] In February 1999, it adopted the Communication *Women and Science: Mobilising Women to Enrich European Research*[7], in which it acknowledged the severe under-representation of women in science and announced an action plan to promote gender equality on three levels: science *by* women, *for* women and *about* women. The priority of the issue was backed by the European Council and Parliament in the form of two resolutions.[8]

The *1999 Action Plan* of the Women and Science Unit within DG Research is organised around two objectives:
- a *Policy Forum* to feed into the policy process and develop collective strategies;
- a *Gender Watch System* to evaluate the EC's goal to promote science by women, science for women and science about women.

As part of the *Policy Forum,* a group of experts was mandated to analyse the current position of female scientists in the European academic world. In 2000 this group, called the *ETAN Working Group on Women and Science* chaired by Prof. M. Osborn from the Max Planck Institute[9], published an extensive report in which gender mainstreaming is identified as a vital precondition for promoting excellence in the science policy of the EU and her member states.[10] The report uncovers important bottlenecks for gender equality in various areas of science and opens the discussion on the role and responsibilities of different actors in science policy, varying from European institutes to national governments, funding agencies and individual universities and research institutes.

Another action taken as part of the *Policy Forum* was the establishment of the so-called *Helsinki Group,* consisting of national civil servant representatives from all countries associated to the Fifth Framework Programme. This group assists the European Commission in collecting statistics and indicators that allow for comparison at European level as well as exchanging experiences and good practices of policy measures that have been implemented at local, regional, national and European levels to encourage women's participation in scientific research. The Helsinki Group members have drawn up national reports, which will be gathered and restructured in a *European report on policies implemented in Europe to promote women in science.*[11] In addition, the Women and Science Unit has started to organise a Network of Women's Networks to mobilise women scientists.[12]

The *Gender Watch System*, set up to monitor the impact of the European Commission's Fifth Framework Programme (FP5), consists of two pillars. The first involves promoting women's participation in FP5. To this end, the Commission has set the *target of 40% participation of women* in the implementation and management of its research programmes at all levels. Explicitly mentioned in the Communication are: the Expert Advisory Groups, Expert Evaluation Panels and Programme Monitoring Panels involved in FP5.[13] Formally women's participation in Programme Committees, proposal and projects is outside the 40% target, but they are monitored all the same.

The second pillar of the *Gender Watch System* concerns an evaluation of the gender dimension in the development, management and implementation of FP5. To this end the Commission has assigned a network of seven research teams to perform *gender impact assessment studies* of all thematic and horizontal programmes within FP5. These studies will investigate the participation of women at all levels of FP5 and give an answer to the question whether the research themes, methods and issues prioritised in FP5 affect women and men differently as well as indicating what can be done to ensure that women's and men's interests are equally served by the programme. The conclusions, which will be published in November 2001,[14] are meant to feed the preparation and implementation of the next community programme for research and technology.

1.1.3 Gender mainstreaming in science: which issues are at stake?

The European Commission's *Women and Science* initiatives are promising in the sense that they approach equal opportunities from various angles. The division that is made between science *by* women, *for* women and *about* women illustrates clearly that different kinds of issues are at stake in the process of promoting equal opportunities in scientific knowledge-building. Equal opportunity policies should not be limited to matters of human resources management and organisational barriers to women's advancement in science, but should also concentrate on the themes and methods that are dealt with: firstly, why are they prioritised and, secondly, do these priorities equally reflect the needs, interests and experiences of women and men?

The slogan of the Commission is perhaps slightly misleading in suggesting that the *Women and Science* initiatives are solely concentrated on women. Actually, they are about gender: they take into account the opportunities of women as well as men and analyse how they relate to each other, something which is most explicitly expressed in the Gender Impact Assessments as performed on FP5. Similarly, gender relations, rather than women's issues, are the prior matter of concern in this manual. In some cases, however, the focus will be explicitly directed towards women. At times, singling out women as the main target group of equal opportunity policies is valuable – if not necessary – to give the process of gender mainstreaming an extra impulse and resolve arrears that cannot be solved otherwise.

Gender mainstreaming as perceived in this manual concerns the whole academic institution and all its activities. When referring to 'science' we do not mean science in the narrow sense of the word – the so-called 'hard sciences' to which the term usually refers in Anglo Saxon universities – but rather all academic endeavours, including arts and philosophy. Gender equality is to be integrated in all the core businesses of academic institutes – in this manual distinguished as research, education and linking science and society – as well as the administrative and managerial structures that enable them to perform their key tasks. In all these structures, gender biases could be at work.

1.1.4 Who should get involved?

The actors involved in gender mainstreaming are all persons in the organisation normally involved in policy making. In universities and academic institutes these are academic leaders, managers and policy makers, working in various faculties, departments and service units, both at central university level and decentralised levels. This has the major advantage that gender mainstreaming is practised by people who are well-acquainted with every aspect of the organisation. Tools and measures for promoting gender mainstreaming can be directly attuned to the contexts in which they are applied.

This does not suggest, however, that you do not need to set up an infrastructure to implement gender mainstreaming in your organisation. Just like any other policy, mainstreaming needs to be initiated, coordinated and controlled. Even though the actual execution rests upon the whole organisation, the strategy needs to be carried out by people who are formally responsible and accountable. Depending on the organisational structure of your institute, these may be individual officers in all units of the university or a bureau or expertise centre at central university level.

1.1.5 Principles of gender mainstreaming

The philosophy that underlies gender mainstreaming is based on *four general principles* that give the strategy its transforming capacity. They challenge you to regard your organisation and its people from a new perspective. Rather than perceiving your institute as an isolated entity – with given purposes and according conditions around which people have to organise their lives – gender mainstreaming urges you to explicitly situate your organisation within a social context. The principles can be summarised as follows.[15]

1. Regarding individuals as whole persons

Employees are not just men and women in their work context. Each individual, either male or female, has different *roles*, different *aspirations* and different *abilities*, both in and outside the workplace. Treating employees as whole persons implies taking into account these aspects in their labour conditions. This can be achieved by facilities like work-life balancing measures – flexible working hours, part-time arrangements, child care facilities, parental and compassionate leave – and offering time, room and space for lifelong learning. The labour environment should be organised in such a way that it does not positively sanction work-attitudes like presenteeism and the 'long hours culture' that still flourish in so many academic institutes.

2. A commitment to democracy

Despite the fact that commitment from the top is important as it comes to implementing a mainstreaming strategy, it can never be imposed as a top-down decision. All actors normally involved in policy making are supposed to embrace this strategy in their own behaviour and activities. Their involvement can be enlarged by installing facilities for participation and consultation, such as councils, committees, networks or centres of expertise. Moreover, democracy entails transparency in procedures and outcomes: e.g. of appointment and promotion procedures, research funding, and pay packages as well as striving towards a gender balance in all decision-making bodies.[16]

3. A drive to social justice

Gender mainstreaming starts with recognising that the university as it exists today is – just like any other organisation – shaped by structures, procedures and policies which contain discriminating elements or at least have discriminatory effects. Gender mainstreaming expresses the will to 'review' these elements in order to eliminate existing inequalities. Fairness, justice and equity are meant to become a natural part of the way things are done in your organisation.

4. Dignity and respect for diversity

Last but not least, gender mainstreaming demands that all staff members are approached with respect and dignity, irrespective of their sex or any other aspect of their social background. By focusing on gender rather than on sex, gender mainstreaming acknowledges that women and men are not homogeneous groups. The differences between them are numerous, e.g. in terms of race, ethnic origin, age, disability, sexual orientation, linguistic or cultural background. Respecting diversity means not judging people on the base of one-sided norms and criteria, but valuing their different perspectives and competences as fruitful additional potentials. All forms of discrimination, harassment or bullying are unacceptable and have to be dealt with firmly.

1.1.6 How does gender mainstreaming relate to other equal opportunities policies?

Gender mainstreaming is innovative in the sense that it proceeds where other equal opportunity strategies stop: it picks up issues that have not been dealt with before. But a comparison between the strategies illustrates that it can never fully replace the traditional equal opportunity models. The following distinction between 'tinkering', 'tailoring' and 'transforming the mainstream' is derived from the work of Prof. T. Rees.[17]

1. Tinkering

Tinkering refers to the first and oldest strategies for promoting equal opportunities of women and men: pursuing *equal rights and equal treatment*. The aim of these strategies is establishing *formal equality* between the sexes. Tinkering refers to the effort to update, mutually attune and fill up the wholes of existing legislation and procedures. A solid legal base and adequate mechanisms to ensure law enforcement are basic prerequisites for the emancipation of subordinated groups in society. They provide a ground to appeal to in cases of direct discrimination, but are by no means sufficient guarantees for *actual* equality between the sexes.[18]

2. Tailoring

Tailoring strategies seek to address the persistent inequalities as described above by establishing specific measures and facilities for women. These are also known as *positive action and positive discrimination* measures. The task of designing and co-ordinating these measures is usually assigned to equal opportunity officers or centres. Rather than formal equality, tailoring strategies pursue *material equality*: they try to promote equality of outcome by equalising starting positions. Positive discrimination goes further in this respect than positive action.

While positive action mainly consists of temporary facilities for women to bridge existing disparities – such as women – only training courses or reintegration programmes – positive discrimination considers such backing facilities insufficient. It states that equal treatment strengthens and maintains existing power relations, since it does not take into account the different circumstances in which women and men are situated. Positive discrimination pursues different treatment in different circumstances to ensure not only equality of access, but also equality of outcome. Familiar examples are quotas and preferential treatment of female candidates in selection and promotion procedures.

An objection to tailoring strategies is that they stimulate women to enter into systems and organisations as they are. Women are supposed to assimilate into the status quo that, in itself, is not under discussion.

Gender inequalities are mainly perceived as women's problems, rather than as issues that concern the organisation as a whole.

3. Transforming the mainstream

Rather than seeking to fit women into the systems and structures as they are, *gender mainstreaming* pursues a reorganisation of universities in such a way that the demands and expectations of women and men are heard and respected equally. This involves more than eliminating discriminatory elements from existing structures, procedures and customs. In mainstreaming, the *transformation* of institutions becomes the agenda. Gender mainstreaming pursues a situation in which all policies are informed by knowledge of the diverse needs and perspectives of their beneficiaries, either male or female.

The institution of science, as it exists today, offers limited room for individual differences between people. Of course, individuals are free to choose any study domain they want. But as soon as they diverge from the prevailing norms and patterns – e.g. by choosing an atypical work-life balance, or analysing reality from a paradigm that radically differs from the accepted point of view – they encounter hurdles that hinder their progress unless they are blessed with highly open-minded superiors or a large supportive network. These hurdles are not exclusively disadvantageous to women, but women encounter them more persistently than men do. Through its aim to resolve them, gender mainstreaming has the potential to enlarge the freedom of movement and thought for all scientists.

As should be clear, gender mainstreaming is a long-term process that entails a complete rethinking of how university systems are shaped. All along this transformation process, tinkering and tailoring strategies need to be continued. The chronological aspect in the approaches as set out above does not imply that one automatically follows the other, or that gender mainstreaming would replace the pursuit of equal rights or positive action. In fact, such restitution might well be counter-productive: as the following framework points out, the strategies focus on different dimensions of equality which are all important in themselves.

Overview of Equal Opportunities Strategies

	Tinkering	**Tailoring**	**Transforming the mainstream**
	Equal rights *Equal treatment*	*Positive action* *Positive discrimination*	*Gender mainstreaming*
Main purpose	Formal equality	Material equality	Gender equality
Major focus	Legislation, formal rules and procedures	Specific problem areas, wherein women are underrepresented or occupy disadvantaged positions	The organisation as a whole with all its structures, values, customs, and policy practices
Strategies	Making sure that men and women are treated equally in all formal rules and procedures Establishing mechanisms to ban all forms of discrimination	Positive action: providing supportive facilities for women to compensate for their unequal starting positions Positive discrimination: preferential treatment for women to ensure not only equality of access, but also equality of outcome	Removing obvious and invisible barriers by incorporating a gender perspective in all policies, structures, procedures and practices Transforming the institution to increase the room for different lifestyles, perspectives and competences – irrespective of gender or any other social dimension
Main actors	Legislative authorities, all persons responsible for establishing official rules and procedures	Special units, committees or officers for equal opportunities	All actors normally involved in policy making, supported by specialised units, centres or officers with specific gender mainstreaming tasks

1.2 WHY IS GENDER MAINSTREAMING A KEY TO SUCCES?

1.2.1 Current changes and challenges in the academic world

Modern universities are confronted with a number of changes inside and outside the academic world that will alter and shape their role and position in society. Probably one of the most challenging developments is the ongoing trend towards globalisation. In the European Union there is a structural move towards developing a European context for research and education. In its policy document *'Making a Reality of the European Research Area: Guidelines for EU Research Activities'*, the European Commission makes a case for making better use of national-based centres of excellence.[19] It warns of the fact that Europe's investments in research and development are dramatically lower than those of the US and Japan. As research is a central element in the emergence and worldwide development of a knowledge-based society, structural changes need to take place in the organisation and culture of European-based research.

The competitiveness that accompanies these processes is also perceptible in academic education. A signal of this direction is the 'Anglo-Saxon turn' in the European-wide endorsement of the Bachelor-Master system, promoting flexibility and mobility among students. The struggle for students that is fed by the increasing social demand for high educated citizens stimulates a search for attractive educational approaches and teaching methods, electronic learning and international classrooms, flexible and contract courses and, finally, international exchange facilities. Implementing these new approaches demands flexibility and puts the traditional educational systems of universities under pressure.

1.2.2 Gender mainstreaming as an engine for innovation

Developments like these reflect opportunities for gender mainstreaming. As they urge universities to make strategic choices and develop new policy lines they provide an excellent chance to incorporate gender perspectives right from the start into new policies. But the reverse is true as well: gender mainstreaming can assist you in developing a reflective and pro-active attitude that enables you to respond quickly to internal and external changes. It may function as an engine to start innovation in your organisation.

The following paragraphs provide some examples of challenges that universities have to meet to maintain their leading roles as knowledge-building and knowledge-transferring institutes. Solving the bottlenecks they cause is not always easy: it may involve a rethinking of the structures, customs and practices that have shaped academic practices for many years. Gender mainstreaming can guide you through this process by its drive to transform thought and behaviour. The principles of diversity, democracy, social justice and treatment of individuals as whole persons urge you to review your organisation and all its activities from within the social context to which it is inexorably linked.

1.2.3 The rise of the powerhouse model

1. Challenges in academic research: specialisation, hybridisation and flexibility

During recent decades the rise of the knowledge society has caused an enormous expansion of academic research practices. The rationalisation of scientific production gave rise to some far-reaching changes in the organisation of university-based research. In many countries government funding for research is divided up between universities and (national) research funding institutions, the latter ensuring that more programmatic research is carried out on a more competitive basis. Along with this division the peer review system has become of central importance and is considered to be the best way to ensure impartial evaluations of quality in academic research.

To further enhance competitiveness, public research funding given to universities is increasingly linked to output-oriented criteria, e.g. concerning the number of publications and citations. At the same time, universities have – either voluntarily or otherwise – started to look for research funding in the marketplace and vice versa. The concept of a common 'Europe' has also stimulated the development of international research groups or networks. More and more commercial institutions are founded in relation to university-based research groups giving rise to a growing need for flexible labour relations to deal with contract research.

In view of these developments universities are likely to become more and more like powerhouses, delivering researchers on demand. The urge for rationalisation and specialisation in the production of science feeds the expectation that a very diverse landscape of universities is going to emerge in the European area. Some institutes will focus perhaps exclusively on fundamental research funded by national research foundations while others will concern themselves merely with practical, policy and business-oriented research.

2. Work-life balancing, democracy and differentiated quality norms

All these changes ask for a reconsideration of current standards and practices in the academic world. How can universities be attractive employer organisations and at the same time cope with the growing competition? How can employees deal with the growing hybridism of their research assignments, sometimes involved in fundamental research, while, at other times, executing market-based research projects? The principles of gender mainstreaming concerning respect for diversity and treating individuals as whole persons will help you to find answers to these questions. In Chapter Three (§ People Management & § People Results), various strategies will pass the review that enable you to develop career prospects and labour conditions in which different backgrounds, aspirations and competences are valued and respected while, at the same time, promoting flexibility and specialisation.

Another urgent matter concerns the protection of the intellectual independence of scientists now that the relationship between science and society becomes more intense. An essential condition to deal with this challenge is breaking the artificial dualism between objectivity and demand-oriented research that currently hinders a constructive debate about this subject. Gender mainstreaming provides you with strong arguments to break this dualism. By uncovering gender biases in the current body of knowledge it proves that all forms of knowledge are socially, culturally and historically constructed (Chapter Two, § Gender Proofing). Rather than distracting academic agenda setting from the realm of the political, gender mainstreaming calls for a democratic discussion about the distribution of resources in science, including business and society-based funding (Chapter Three, § Partners and Resources).

Finally, mainstreaming promotes the development of the university as a powerhouse by pursuing to break one-dimensional definitions of quality. Thus, it clears the way for an increased specialisation among scientists. If this diversity is combined with a culture of democracy it is likely to positively affect the quality of research itself: it contributes to more pluralism in scientific approaches. The history of science shows that interaction between scientists of various backgrounds can give an impulse to innovative approaches, insights and research questions.[20]

1.2.4 The growing demand for flexible and knowledgeable citizens

1. Challenges in academic education: allowing for diversity and flexibility

Since the 1970s all European universities have been confronted with an increasing participation of students. In response to society's need for more highly educated people universities have become mass educational institutes. To promote demand-oriented and performance-based teaching, public funding for education has increasingly been linked to numbers of students and graduates. These developments have strengthened the competition for students among universities.

Stimulated by the demand for flexible and knowledgeable citizens as well as the concept of life-long learning this competitiveness in education has posed new challenges regarding curricular change and new forms of teaching. Digital and distant learning are not just concepts for Open Universities anymore but are also being introduced in regular university education as well. At the same time there is the establishment of special 'University Colleges' in many universities in which the personal contact between teacher and student is restored. New teaching methods are designed to make students responsible for their own learning process, something that is increasingly problem-based instead of purely disciplinary. As for the curriculum, there is a demand for postgraduate courses as well as for more general and interdisciplinary education.

2. Creating an attractive working environment for a diversity of students

By promoting (gender) diversity in educational programmes, methods, institutes and ways of addressing students you can establish a learning environment in which a broad range of talents can flourish. It enables students to explore their own ways, follow their specific interests, develop competences in ways that suit them and meet their diverse needs for coaching and mentorship.[21]

A precondition for creating such an environment is a gender balance among the scientific staff involved in developing and executing educational programmes (Chapter Two, § Organisation & Implementation). A variety of role models will have a positive effect on transforming the traditional image of science. It would also be advisable to incorporate diversity in the classroom as an issue in training and competence building trajectories (Chapter Two, § Building Awareness). These enable educational staff members to satisfy a variety of demands and expectations, both of female and male students, with respect to teaching methods and the content of the curriculum. Above all, gender mainstreaming in academic education requires a thorough reflection on the existing male hegemony that characterises its language, organisation and delivery (Chapter Two, § Gender Proofing).

1.2.5 The call for accountability and public control

1. Challenges in linking science and society: decentralisation versus public control

Together, the trends as described above – the increasing globalisation, the expansion of research and the onrush of students – have stimulated the development of new management structures in most European universities. The need for flexibility and competitiveness are giving rise to more distanced relationships between governments and universities in many countries. Within universities, faculties and departments often carry responsibility over their own policies and decision-making. Processes of decentralisation, integral management and withdrawal of top-down interference are giving a necessary push towards the development of the university as a powerhouse.

At the same time, the need for accountability and public control has grown, partly fed by the expansion of commercial research practices.

Concepts like the social relevance of research and democratic control over public resources are increasingly gaining importance. As a result, universities are moving towards decentralised autonomous units, bound to central governments by covenants. In the process, quality management, output funding and contract compliance are becoming important features for accountability and public control in modern university management.

2. A drive towards social justice and social relevance

The process model for gender mainstreaming as presented in Chapter Three shows you how gender can be mainstreamed in control mechanisms as mentioned above. By regularly reviewing the people results, customer results, society results, and key performance results of your organisation you can enhance the quality and social relevance of academic practices. Women's voices and experiences may not be denied in this process: they constitute more than half of the population in EU member states. By denying their perspectives and interests you run the risk of dissatisfying an increasingly influential group of employees, students and social partners (Chapter Three, § Results).

Currently, women's under-representation in science – and more specifically in decision-making on science policy – limits their opportunity to introduce their points of view in setting the academic research and education agenda. By promoting women's participation in science you will not only enhance social justice but also enhance the social relevance of research practices. A study on the labour market perspectives of young scientists in the Netherlands showed that women tend to be more attached to values with respect to social relevance of research practices than men.[22]

1.2.6 The need of pro-active strategies in human resources management

1. Challenges in HRM: personnel shortages and growing competition

Within the next few years universities are likely to face a shortage of academic personnel due to the continuous economic growth, the increasing labour market demand for academic grades and the impending 'retirement flow'. This flow will strike most fiercely in senior positions. At the same time, academic institutes are confronted with an increasing competition for good researchers in the (international) academic arena. A growing number of countries in and outside the EU are relying on economic structures that are mainly dependent on the knowledge infrastructure. Led by the US, they are lining up to attract excellent graduates from all over the world.[23]

European universities are challenged to prevent a brain-drain of talented and ambitious scientists. An increasing number of young potentials are crossing over to foreign academic institutes, especially to the US. The high salaries in this region hinder European universities to recruit talented post-docs in return.[24] On top of this, European universities face a decreasing appeal for scientific careers among academic students and graduates that may well strengthen the impending lack of academic personnel. All these developments call for immediate action to improve attractive career prospects and labour conditions in science.[25]

2. The female potential: an essential resource to promote quality in science

To be able to draw on a balanced and sufficiently qualified pool of scientists, now and in the future, universities urgently have to develop proactive HRM-strategies. In this respect, female scientists constitute a potential that is insufficiently utilised. During the past decennia women in the EU member states have rapidly caught up in the field of academic education. Overall, the number of male and female students and graduates gets more and more balanced, though this picture varies extensively between individual disciplines.

Universities as employers do not optimally utilise this increasing female academic potential. Despite the fact that female students tend to graduate faster and with better results than male students do, the share of female research assistants is significantly lower than that of female graduates in most countries. Women that do start a scientific career are usually confronted with slower career paths and have higher turnover rates than their male colleagues.[26] Women's share in scientific posts rapidly drops with each step upwards in the career system. (See: Illustration, Scissors Diagram, p.X)

In Chapter Three, several HRM-strategies are presented to optimise the utilisation of female talents in science. Two examples of barriers for women's progress that urgently need to be addressed are, firstly, the reliance on informal networks for advancing in academic careers[27] and, secondly, blurred selection criteria and recruitment procedures.[28] But in order to ensure a high quality of academic personnel universities should not resort to HRM-strategies alone.

During the past decades, the causes of the relatively slow career path and quick departure of female scientists have been extensively studied by researchers all over the EU. The answers to the question 'Why so slow?'[29] show large similarities, despite some national differences in university structures. A myriad of cultural and organisational factors appears to play a role, such as norms with respect to full-time availability[30], demands of international working experience[31] and the quality of mentorship and coaching practices by superiors[32]. This indicates that utilising the potential that female scientists have to offer requires a wide transformation of the academic working environment. It demands resolving a broad range of barriers embedded in university systems and structures as well as pursuing a situation in which men and women are able to live and work according to their own values and ambitions. In other words: it demands gender mainstreaming.

1.2.7 Managerial challenges

1. The tension between research and teaching

For universities and their core activities the evolution towards specialisation and the development of distinctive profiles in research and teaching programmes to be competitive in the academic and research market puts the long-standing interconnection between research and teaching on the line. More and more both objectives are based on different financial resources whereas both processes demand increasingly different infrastructures within the organisation. Also, the professional skills and competences of the people in education and in research differ. From *an organisational and management perspective* it would be easier to professionalise and separate the diverse policies, strategies and staff management focused on either research or education. From *an academic viewpoint*, however, the separation of research and education poses a serious threat for the quality of both scientific research and education. It is a challenge for management in universities to concentrate on the connection between these two core businesses while at the same time coping with the demands of more distinctive or specialised teaching and research practices.[33]

2. Academic leadership: the tension between business and academic paradigm

Changes like the scaling up of universities, the need to create distinct profiles in research and teaching and the need for centres of expertise built on excellent internationally trained researchers have created a university that is an ever more complex organisation. They stress the urge of promoting professional and flexible management. Until today, however, most of the management staff in universities have been academics rather than management or business experts.

Academic leaders currently experience an ongoing clash between two paradigms: firstly, the business paradigm that implies a total reorganisation of financial resources, human resources, policy and strategic management and eventually research as such and, secondly, the academic, scientific paradigm.[34] Some professors are already solely active in those research fields that are funded by industries and commercial businesses or are using external non-governmental money-flows to sponsor their entire activities. They are like young entrepreneurs in the academic field. The start-up and successful business results of several spin-offs from universities, accomplished by academic professors, are another illustration of this trend. Other academics, however, cherish the principles of academic freedom, impartial research and the intimate relationship between research and academic training.

Illustration

In recent debates with professors of different faculties at the K.U. Leuven it turned out that one of their major concerns was the shift in their duties and responsibilities from scholar to manager. Although the job-profile, job-vacancies and selection criteria for their functions have, as yet, not been adapted they are deeply affected by this shift. The professors feel they are confronted with a dilemma in their work situation. Considering themselves to be researchers in the first place, their management tasks do not allow them enough time to fulfil their academic duties to their satisfaction. The organisation wants them to be top-managers, but they lack the skills of 'managers', for the simple fact that they are just not trained as such. On top of this, the faculties' logistics and administration are not yet adapted to this new situation so that full-professors have to spend a lot of time executing organisational and even administrative tasks.[35]

3. Gender mainstreaming: a process model for promoting flexible management

The tensions described above are only two examples of challenges that put the current management structures in universities under pressure. Universities are faced with the challenge to develop flexible and reflexive management models which can cope with the tensions embedded in the core businesses of universities and, at the same time, can cope with external developments that alter and change their role in society. The process model for gender mainstreaming in academic management as presented in Chapter Three is a proper model to promote such flexibility.

The chapter stimulates you to start focusing on quality management, stressing not only the university's output in terms of teaching results, research, and technologies, but also the management processes that support their very existence. By mainstreaming gender equality into the EFQM-model of excellence, the chapter shows how you can promote a smooth internal operation and external proliferation of your organisation, without loosing sight of matters like quality and social justice.

Before presenting this transforming process model, we will focus on the university structures as they are now. In the next chapter (Chapter Two) an overview of instruments is presented that enable you to apply gender mainstreaming to your university. Divided over four categories, they stimulate you to review current practices in research, education, and linking science and society. Together, they show you how to mobilise people all the way through your organisation to embrace the principles of gender mainstreaming.

CHAPTER 2
GENDER MAINSTREAMING AT UNIVERSITIES: THE INSTRUMENTAL APPROACH

2.1 A WAY TO INTRODUCE GENDER MAINSTREAMING

This chapter will offer a *framework* for introducing the gender main-streaming policy, that is, integrating the gender equality perpective into the *core activities* of knowledge-organisations. In this respect universities are looked at from a rather classical perspective, revolving around providing education, conducting scientific research and linking science and society. The status quo in these three core businesses is questioned, especially as the existing structures and cultures in universities proved gender biased.

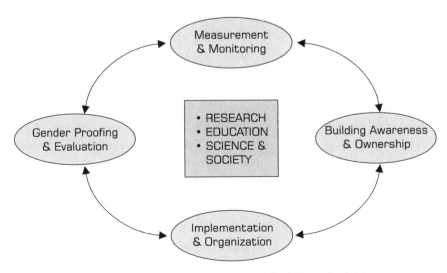

Gender Mainstreaming Process in Universities' Core Activities

Gender mainstreaming will be introduced through the presentation of four toolkits or sets of instruments. These toolkits consist of *Measurement and Monitoring, Implementation and Organisation, Building Awareness and Ownership,* and *Gender Proofing and Evaluation.* The presented sets of instruments are easy to use by anyone in the organisation and to different extents. That is to say, that depending on your *position and function* in the university, you can apply them according to *the utility, the possibility and the opportunity* they offer you in your gender mainstreaming efforts. It is important to notice that the presentation of those four different toolkits does not imply an order of any kind. You can use them in a random order.

Example

Being responsible for the teaching matters in your faculty, you think for example that lots of actions and measures concerning equal opportunities have been introduced already in the educational curriculum. You want to know if these actions have had any repercussions. Is there is a growing gender-awareness among the faculty members and the students? You can apply elements from the toolkit as it is deployed under the heading 'gender proofing and evaluation for education'.

---

1. Measurement and Monitoring

Systematic collection and dissemination of data on the position and opportunities of women and men is indispensable to assess which areas most urgently need to be addressed and check the impact of policies and measures that have been implemented. The long-term effect of gender mainstreaming cannot be measured directly, but gender mainstreaming consists of various, mutually attuned actions in different policy areas, which can and should be measured separately. To prevent discouragement and apathy, even small successes need to be acknowledged by stressing the notion that gender mainstreaming derives its power from a cumulation of small results.[36]

2. Gender Proofing and Evaluation

The process of gender mainstreaming is not based on empirical data alone. Measurement is very useful to indicate the existence of inequalities between the sexes, such as disparities in access and representation. However, it can not uncover what the causes of these inequalities are. Likewise, monitoring tools are useful to check whether progress has been booked towards gender equality, but they can not sort out whether this progress has been achieved by structural transformations of the mainstream. This is where the process of gender proofing becomes effective. Gender proofing tools are designed to trace the causes of existing gender biases, and provide guidelines for changing structures and procedures aiming at promoting gender diversity.

3. Implementation and Organisation

At all levels of the organisation, persons have to be assigned who are officially responsible and accountable for gender mainstreaming: people who initiate, implement, and co-ordinate the process. Preferably, these are academic leaders and managers, who are in a position to influence policy practices and decisions. Gender mainstreaming strategies will not be effective as long as they are simply 'added' to the portfolio of individual managers and policy makers. Specific training and sufficient financial means are required.

4. Building Awareness and Ownership

Gender mainstreaming implies a paradigm shift in thinking of all actors involved in policy making, especially of academic leaders and managers who are officially assigned to initiate and co-ordinate the process. This requires training to reach a certain degree of gender awareness and gender expertise. Training thus enables relevant policy makers to dismantle seemingly gender-neutral practices and transform them, meeting the demands of a broad range of people, women as well as men. Apart from a certain degree of expertise it is necessary that gender mainstreaming is taken on board as an administrative and management responsibility in its own right.

The provided sets of tools can be used as a step-by-step guide throughout the different phases of integrating equality into the whole academic agenda. It can be consulted when confronted with a specific gender related topic in your organisation or used in a specific phase of integrating equality into a certain activity domain of your organisation (teaching, research or linking science and society). The tools are not meant to be exhaustive. They are merely indicative for all actors involved in one or another phase of the gender mainstreaming process. For as far as real tested instruments or gender indicators are available, these will be worked out in more detail. The practical use of the possible tools will be illustrated by good practices.

2.2 THE TOOLKITS AT WORK IN A GOOD PRACTICE CASE[37]

To illustrate the practical functioning of the sets of instruments and tools a good practice business-case will accompany you in your reading. The case tells the story of the professional services firm *Deloitte & Touche*, realising in 1991 that the high turnover of high-qualified and talented women harmed their business success. The way they detected the problem, looked for solutions, installed gender equality policies, and were finally able to transform some discriminating features in their business culture and procedures, provide a perfect overall illustration of the logic of the instruments and tools presented.

Before introducing specific measures concerning gender equality in their firm, *Deloitte & Touche* went through different phases. *Firstly*, the so-called 'Women's Initiative' installed a task force (implementation and organisation) to detect the bottlenecks in women's careers (measurement and monitoring), to organise workshops and training and to clear the way for installing a tailor-made gender equality program. *Secondly*, they made sure everyone in management got informed about gender mechanisms in the organisation (awareness building) and every manager in the firm was shown his or her responsibility in creating a more gender equal workplace (ownership). Throughout this process, activities and practices that were common among the firm's partners and that were deeply rooted in the organisational culture were assessed and evaluated with respect to their gender impact (gender proofing and evaluation).

This all happened in 1991. Nine years later, the present CEO[38] of *Deloitte Consulting*, states:

"We've not only narrowed the gender gap, we've narrowed the gap between who we think we are and who we really are. Now, when I say ours is a meritocracy, I'm speaking about men and women. It's not easy to manage a diverse group of people. We have to be creative and flexible in developing coaching and mentoring capabilities. Although the Women's Initiative has made managing more complicated, the benefits are substantial: greater creativity, faster growth and far greater performance for our clients."[39]

Parts of the story of Deloitte & Touche will be presented throughout the text as a practical illustration of the gender mainstreaming process by means of 'instruments' similar to the presented tools of Measurement and Monitoring, Implementation and Organisation, Awareness Building and Ownership and Gender Proofing and Evaluation.

2.3 GENDER MAINSTREAMING: THE INSTRUMENTAL APPROACH

2.3.1 Measurement and Monitoring

1. Do your data reveal gender (in)equalities?

Measurement and monitoring refer to the collection of gender-disaggregated data in your organisation, and the follow-up on these findings. In order to establish a systematic 'state of the art' on the gender relations in your university, these data-gatherings need to be taken over time. The measurements collected in the process of monitoring are of a quantitative nature, like facts and figures, tables, equations, comparisons, etcetera. Monitoring qualitative data, like the collection and interpretation of personal stories and in-depth interviews, will be dealt with more extensively in the 'gender proofing and evaluation'-process. However, as the flowchart on the working of the four instruments shows, they are interrelated (see above). The more the cyclic process is gone through – in any order you choose – the more information about the gender equality in your organisation is gained, and the closer your organisation is to achieving the goals of gender mainstreaming.

2. What can you achieve with measurement and monitoring?

Why would you go through all the trouble of collecting data on the gender-relations in your organisation?

The attached fragment from the *Deloitte & Touche* case is illustrative for the importance of gender disaggregated data collection. More specific, the gathered data give a clear view on the horizontal segregation in the firm.

Deloitte & Touche Best Practice

"Since the fastest way to change behaviours is to measure them, the task force started by *simply asking for numbers*. Beginning in 1993, in the midst of the workshops, local offices were asked to conduct annual reviews to determine if the top-rated women were receiving their proportionate share of the best assignments. Some offices resisted, questioning the usefulness of this time consuming exercise or fearing that the initiative would lead to quotas. However, a few pointed phone calls from the CEO prodded the laggards. The reviews confirmed our suspicions: women tended to be assigned to projects in non-profit, health care and retail, segments that generally lacked large global accounts, while men received most of the assignments in manufacturing, financial services and highly visible areas like mergers and acquisitions."[40]

This is only one example of the usefulness of measurement and monitoring. The instrument serves at least a twofold purpose. The collection of gender disaggregated data can be seen *firstly* as an informative instrument, and *secondly* as a strategic one.

1. The informative purpose of measurement and monitoring

By measurement and monitoring, you find out where exactly in the organisation women are underrepresented or indeed overrepresented. It allows you to take stock of the gender relations in your organisation. Facts and figures give an indication of *the bottlenecks and hurdles* women experience throughout their academic careers, and at which point in their career women experience the glass ceiling for example. Gender disaggregated statistics also show *the extent* of the existing segregation. Problem areas can be identified immediately. Monitoring in time finally gives you information on the organisational *trends* in these gender-relations. When systematically collected, the comparability of data is invreased. Besides ensuring the gender disaggregation of all your statistics it is important to develop specific indicators to measure gender differences.

2. The strategic purpose of measurement and monitoring

Data on the position of women give you *an instrument to influence the policy-agenda* of your university. Once you can show the underrepresentation of women as a real problem, supported by (statistical) data, you have a stronger case when you want to put gender equality on the agenda. On top of that, gender disaggregated statistics can function as a *management tool*. In the area of *human resources management*, gender monitoring is of great importance. Data highlight problem domains within academic careers, and deliver priority-lists and other input for specific human resources policies. When the university is already involved in equal opportunities policies, gender disaggregated statistics can function as an instrument of *public relation management*. As gender-biased structures and cultures are invreasingly recognised as counterproductive in knowledge-organisations, positive trends can attract diverse and highly qualified academics, and can install a better image towards the broader society and potential customers. Finally, gender mainstreaming implies that gender specific measurement and monitoring is *part of the evaluation process* of existing policies of any kind, and especially of equal opportunities policies. Similarly, monitoring statistics can form the basis for setting *equality targets*. In both ways statistics provide a useful management tool by which the progress towards more equal opportunities can be measured.[41]

Deloitte & Touche Best Practice

"The task force prepared the firm for change by laying a foundation of data, including personal stories. Deloitte was doing a great job of hiring high-performing women. In fact, women often earned higher performance ratings than men in their first years with the firm. Yet, the percentage of women decreased with every step up the career ladder, in all practices and regions, and many women left the firm just when they were expected to receive promotions. Interviews with current and former women professionals explained why. Most weren't leaving to raise families. They had weighted their options in Deloitte's male-dominated culture and found them wanting. Many of them, dissatisfied with the culture they perceived as endemic to professional services firms, switched professions. And all of them together represented a major lost opportunity for the firm. These facts made for a sobering report to the senior partners of the firm's management committee in 1993."[42]

---

3. Tools for measurement and monitoring in knowledge-organisations

When you start gathering gender-disaggregated statistics and quantitative data in your university, four questions can be of help for structuring the collected data.

1. What data provide me information on the equality of *access and opportunities*?
2. What data do I need for measuring the equality of *participation*?
3. What data provide me information on the equality of *outcome*?
4. What data provide me information on the equality of *condition*?

The four questions refer to the different objectives of an equality approach. Data on the equality of *access and opportunities* can reveal factors that prevent men and women from accessing and advancing in all domains of academic life on an equal basis. Data on the equality of *participation* can reveal for example that resources are not divided evenly, or that excluding criteria are at work, criteria that don't follow the logic and culture of achievement and performance (e.g. age-criteria). The third data on the equality of *outcome*, refer to achieving overall equality between different groups in university. Do women, for example, stand equal chances to men when applying for research funding? Finally, data on the equality of *condition* can show the extent to which men and women are paid equally, or map the extent to which the organisation render different conditions according to the different needs, aspirations and roles of its people. They contain information about male and female pay grading systems (e.g. secretaries versus technicians).[43]

1. Monitoring tools for measuring equality in *access and opportunities*

- percentage of women starting university studies (per discipline)
- percentage of women getting a Bachelor's degree (per discipline)
- percentage of women getting a Masters' degree (per discipline)

- percentage of women starting a PhD (per discipline)
- percentage of women starting a post-doctoral project (per discipline)
- percentage of women assistant professors – women associated professors – women full professors (per discipline)

2. Monitoring tools for measuring equality in *participation*

- Concerning participation in scientific positions:
  - percentage of tenured women (per discipline)
  - gender-disaggregated age-figures of scientific personnel in the different stages of the academic career (especially on the crucial moments in academic careers: appointments, promotions, etc)
  - proportion of male and female scientific personnel in researching activities versus teaching and administration activities
  - gender-disaggregated worktime-tables for the three core-activities. Percentage time spent by male and female professors on teaching versus researching activities and other activities (e.g. student and faculty guidance, administration, patient care, etc)
  - percentage of women staff at each level of the academic hierarchy (undergraduates, Ph.D.-students, research assistants, assistant professors, associate professors, full professors)
  - percentage of women applicants for new appointments (yearly and at each level of the academic career)
  - percentage of women science professionals in the private and public sector versus participation of women scientists in universities

- Concerning participation in the university's policy-making offices:
  - gender-balance in academic management positions (e.g. university board, university committees, etc)
  - participation of women in decentralised decision making offices (e.g. deans, faculty board, appointment commissions, etc)
  - percentage of women in scientific versus non-scientific staff

- Concerning participation in resources
  - money-flows towards the different faculties, offices, research units, etc (linked to rate of male/female scientists in these faculties, offices and units)
  - the amount of funding by research councils and similar grant awarding and research funding institutions (percentage per discipline linked to the presence of male/female scientists in these disciplines)
  - gender-disaggregated statistics on participation in the boards and committees of research councils and similar grant awarding and research funding organisations

– gender of referees for peer review, exercises and activities

3. Monitoring tools for measuring equality in *outcome*

- percentage of women academics receiving different prizes and awards on different levels (e.g. within the university, national level, international level)
- career-path-data:
  - outcome and results for women who started university-studies (Bachelor's-Masters' degree, ...)
  - outcome and results for women who started their Ph.D. (time worked on it, age-figures, results and grades, ...)
  - outcome and results for women applying for post-doc research funding
  - outcome and results for women applying for new appointments (in relation to the application-rate of women)
- turnover rates, broken down by gender

4. Monitoring tools for measuring equality in *condition*

- percentage of women in the contract staff versus the tenured staff
- percentage of women professors at all levels of the university in the different work-time schedules (part-time, full-time, ...), in the different contracts (short-term, fixed-term, ...)
- gender-disaggregated information about number and duration of career breaks throughout the academic career (e.g. maternity leave, career interruptions, ...)
- composition of the total pay packet at every grade of the academic career and the percentage of women in these different grades (fixed renumeration, possible additional payments, honoraria, ...)
- comparisons of the pay grading systems

None of these data reveal any information in itself. They have to be linked and compared in order to be able to show trends and patterns (e.g. horizontal and vertical segregation).

4. Do's and Don'ts[44]

- Monitoring of measurements *over time* is important and adds up to the quality of statistics. Try to gather the same data every year or more frequently if necessary. Link the gathering to important academic decisions, like at the end of an appointment period.

- Try to gather as *basic statistics* as possible. This makes comparisons with other data, for instance external data, more feasible.
- The above-presented framework is only meant to be a guidance in your collecting activities. Make sure that *all* data you gather in your organisation are broken down by gender. It is relatively easy to do and it can yield lots of interesting information.
- The collection of gender information does not necessarily mean an investment in terms of time and energy. Sometimes the necessary information is *already available* somewhere in the organisation, but rather in the form of raw material. Try to add the gender aspect systematically, in order to get gender disaggregated statistics for the whole of the organisation.
- The mere collection of gender statistics may not be sufficient. In order to utilise the informative and strategic power of statistics, you can try to get them *analysed, commented upon, published and communicated* inside and outside the organisation.
- *Never* publish organisation's data that are not gender-disaggregated!
- The *presentation* of the gender data is very important. Try to present statistics broken down by gender, in such a way that the gender inequality is striking right away (e.g. the scissors diagram, the pyramid system, etc)
- A *comparative approach* towards statistics is recommended. The gender-ratio in other universities, institutes or in industrial companies where women scientists are employed is important in order to make comparisons, analyses and interpretations more accurate.
- Try not to stick to the *horizontal approach* only. This means that you collect gender disaggregated data on every academic position and participation. It is important to map global academic careers, to see how women's and men's careers are developing and where the impediments are situated. Since gender mainstreaming implies 'regarding employees as whole persons' (See Chapter One § Principles of gender mainstreaming) it is recommended to collect some basic *'family'-data* (e.g. birth of children, ...). This is of course more difficult than collecting the data as described above, because this information is often subject to privacy regulations.
- Numbers do not speak for themselves! When statistics are being used as a base for specific policy decisions, it is recommended to let the statistics be handled by someone with *gender knowledge and expertise*. The taking into account of existing differences between men and women concerning their different position in academia, their different academic attitudes and aspirations is of great importance when

drawing 'political' consequences. If one does not approach these differences properly, policies based upon mere statistical information risk confirming and re-enforcing the male dominated gender contract (e.g. the limits that part-time academics – as a measure for balancing life-work – experience in the further development of their careers).

- Following the same logic, the risk of *statistical discrimination* can be outlined. This term refers to the fact that an individual is seen and judged, not as that particular person, but as a member of a group, with the same characteristics, traits and attitudes as that group. In the long run this may lead to the reinforcement of stereotypes instead of raising gender-awareness (e.g. the statistical fact that women leave university more often then their male colleagues, may re-enforce the stereotype that women are less stable in their jobs than men are). Thorough analyses and expert interpretation of this specific statistical fact will show that this is not related to the sex of academics, but to the limited opportunities for women for advancing in their academic careers and a lack of respect universities tend to have for the life-work balance. So, make sure that when you present gender statistics, you have a good view on how these data need to be interpreted, in order to be able to challenge stereotypes of the above kind.

5.   Measurement and monitoring: What are the profits?

The collection of gender-disaggregated statistics is indispensable in the gender mainstreaming process of organisations. It is however an activity of a more supporting nature. Good practices can only be dealt with, in respect to presentation forms, the strategic capacity of statistics and statistics as awareness-raising tools. In general, the measure of setting targets for the representation of women in science is also connected to the statistical monitoring protocol.[45]

Illustration

A good practice illustration concerning the profits of *measurement and monitoring* is the recently published *Just Pay* Report[46] of the Equal Pay Task Force, established in 1999 within the Equal Opportunities Commission (EOC). This Task Force's mission was to explore the issue of the pay gap between men and women in Great Britain. It had to take evidence and make recommendations on how to close that part of the pay gap due to pay discrimination by a specific date.

The report outlines the difficulties concerning defining and measuring the gender pay gap.

'Equal pay is not just about wages and salaries. Part of the complexity surrounding the issue arises out of the increasingly intricate *packages* that employers offer some of their employees. These can include bonuses and overtime, performance related pay, health insurance, cars and training.'[47]

The report provides a lot of recommendations on how to improve measurements and data sources. The explorative nature of the study aside, the Task Force also sets out specific targets on closing the gender pay gap in GB.

'We believe it is perfectly feasible, with concerted action by all the key players, that the gender pay gap due to discrimination in the workplace should be reduced by 50% within the next 5 years and eliminated entirely within 8 years.'[48]

Good Practice

A good practice example on the *presentation form* of measurements and data is the so-called *scissors diagram*. The figure below shows the diagrammed data on the proportion of men and women at each stage of the academic career in Six Member States in 1997.[49]

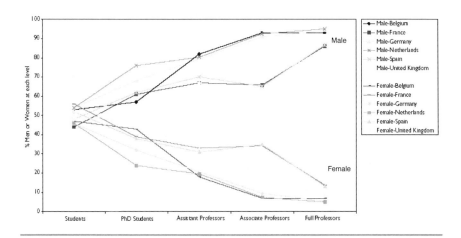

2.3.2 Implementation and Organisation

1. How to make sure gender mainstreaming is for real in your university?

Implementing gender mainstreaming refers to the process of providing a structural and cultural basis for equal opportunities in your university. This structural and cultural embedding of equal opportunities is a critical factor, as the transforming capacity of gender mainstreaming consists of the focusing on systems and structures that create disadvantages for women.[50] Basically, implementing gender mainstreaming means making sure that equal opportunities are institutionalised in the university structures and embedded in its culture. In concreto, it entails the making of all crucial decisions needed in the planning and execution of equal opportunities actions and measures. It includes the planning of objectives, targets and goals to attain the formulation of specific supportive measures, the defining of the roles, responsibilities and accountability of the different actors involved, the setting out of the required inputs (e.g. human resources, time, budgets, gender-expertise) and the mapping of the external factors to be taken into account.[51]

2. Why do you need supportive structures for gender mainstreaming?

Gender equality is a topic that still encounters a lot of resistance within organisations. Therefore, it is not evident to plan, structure and apply measures and actions right away. The importance of *structural planning and – implementation of equal opportunities policies* goes right back to the heart of the gender mainstreaming process itself. Creating appropriate organisational arrangements, in combination with raising awareness, training and expertise, reporting mechanisms, commitment of leaders, incentives to build ownership and accountability and resources are the structural prerequisites of mainstreaming.[52] The development of specific structures concerning equal opportunities (centres of expertise, networks, responsible actors) correlates positively with the *sustainability* of actions and measures. The attribution of executive responsibilities concerning the gender mainstreaming goal increases the chance of lasting equality effects. Making this *accountability* part of someone's performance evaluation increases this positive effect. In this way, *ownership* over the results of measures and actions in the different domains of the organisation is created. Through these processes, *gender awareness* is spread in the organisation, making a positive cultural change more likely. Next to the above opportunities that are created in the process of structural implementation, the outcomes of various practices on gender mainstreaming projects have shown the importance of the above conditions explicitly. All progress reports on mainstreaming activities in the European Union present not only the achievements but also problems related to the lack of one or more of these conditions. They emphasise especially the lack of special budgets for attaining the equality goal is very common.[53] Insufficient systematic structural embedding of actions and measures for improving gender equality often form the basis for the fading out of the expected mainstreaming effect.[54]

The following story of *Deloitte & Touche* provides some good examples of implementation factors that increase the chance of successful organisational and cultural change that is necessary in the process of achieving more equal opportunities.

Deloitte & Touche Best Practice

A Two-Stage Process

"Deloitte's Initiative for the Retention and Advancement of Women grew out of a 1992 **task force** chaired by Mike Cook, then **CEO of Deloitte & Touche**. A number of women partners initially wanted nothing to do with the effort because it implied affirmative action. But Cook, along with a handful of partners, women and men, insisted that high turnover for women was a problem of the outmost urgency. In professional services firms, they argued, the product is talent, billed to the client by the hour, and so much of our firms' product was leaving at an alarming rate. Cook made sure that women and men were part of the task force and that it represented a broad range of views, including outright scepticism. Once in place, the task force didn't immediately launch a slew of new organizational policies aimed at outlawing bad behavior. Instead, it approached the problem methodically, just as we would approach a consulting assignment. Thus, it first investigated the problem and gathered the data necessary to make a business case, not a moral or an emotional one, for change. Then it prepared the groundwork for change by holding a series of intensive, **two-days workshops for all of our management professionals.** These sessions were designed to bring to the surface the gender-based assumptions about careers and aspirations that had discouraged high-performing women from staying. **Only then did the firm announce a series of policies aimed at keeping women. A major component of these policies was to first get all the firm's offices to monitor the progress of their women professionals**. The head of every office received the message that the CEO and other managing partners were watching, and in turn, women started getting their share of premier client assignments and informal mentoring. Other policies, **designed to promote more balance between work and life** for women and men, also helped. These efforts have opened up our work environment and our culture in ways we never expected."[55]

"Like many other managing partners, I began routinely discussing assignment decisions with the partners in charge of project staffing to make sure women had opportunities for key engagements. Most offices began tracking the activities of their high-performing women on a quarterly basis. To complement the connections that men naturally made with one another, we began hosting regular networking events for women, for example panel discussions where women partners discussed their careers and leadership roles, followed by networking receptions. we also started formal career planning for women partners and senior managers. This planning proved so helpful that women suggested men also be included, thus giving rise to Deloitte Consulting's current Partner Development Program. Only after the operational changes had percolated through the organization did the task force introduce clear **accountability** for the changes that were being made. It offered offices a menu of goals derived from the Women's Initiative, such as a recruiting hit rate or a reduction in the gender gap turnover, yet left it up to the offices to pick goals best suited for their particular situations. Office heads started including their choices among the objectives that drove their year-end evaluations and compensation. And the firm made sure that results on turnover, promotion and other key numbers for each office were circulated widely among management, feeding a healthy internal competitiveness. Low-performing offices got calls or visits from task force members to push for better results. Today, partners know that they will not become leaders of this organisation if they have not demonstrated their commitment to the Women's Initiative."[56]

3. Tools for the implementation and organisation of gender mainstreaming

1. Involving thc 'stakeholders': creatlng *commitment*, *responsibility and accountability* of the gender mainstreaming strategy in research, education and scientific services.

One of the underlying principles of mainstreaming is *a commitment to democracy* (see Chapter One, § Principles of gender mainstreaming). Hence, practices of participation, discussion and consultation in the process of implementing an equality policy are expressions of the organisational commitment to this general mainstreaming principle.[57] Ideally, all members of the university should be involved in this dynamic process of developing and implementing gender mainstreaming policies. This is of course hard to achieve and in order to meet this goal anyway, groups of stakeholders with their advocates can be brought together and involved.[58] The involvement of women academics, who are the main beneficiaries of gender mainstreaming actions and measures universities' structures, is extremely important. Their participation (e.g. through networking, participation in decision-making offices, ...) will enforce the relevance, effectiveness and sustainability of the gender mainstreaming policies.[59]

Two main tools for *involving the stakeholders and creating commitment* are:

1. *Activating and maximising participatory mechanisms*
   Representatives from various groups within universities have access to the decision-making process through participatory mechanisms. Activating and maximising these participatory mechanisms in this context means to ensure the participation and contribution of different perspectives, in particular that of female academics, in decision-making about policies and programmes concerning equal opportunities in universities. Activate all participatory bodies (e.g. works council, university- and faculty board, student board) by placing gender mainstreaming on their agenda.

2. *Networking*
   The implementation and monitoring of specific networks give a more structural and cultural basis to the gender mainstreaming approach. Networks challenge the academic agenda in terms of the promotion of equality, work on the commitment from the top, give input from women's views, provide relevant information on equal opportunities and share expertise on gender mainstreaming.

Good Practice

At the K.U.Leuven an *internal network of Mainstreaming Promoters* was established. In every faculty, logistic service and administration of the university, the Faculty Board appointed on voluntary basis a male and female employee for the function of Mainstreaming Promoter.

The Mainstreaming Promoter has the following *responsibilities*[60]:

– *They function as the promoter* of the gender mainstreaming strategy in their faculty or their work and study field. This means that they stand for the horizontal integration of equal opportunities in the daily functioning of their faculty or service.

– They are *contact persons* concerning the equal opportunities communications. For the top-down communication, they are the spokespersons for the Centre of Equal Opportunities Policies (This is the central equal opportunity body) towards the faculties and services. For the bottom-up communication, they guarantee the information-flow from within the faculties and services to this Centre.

– *They promote and monitor all actions and measures* taken in the faculties and the services for which they are responsible.

– They are the intermediary for *the communication and the awareness raising* concerning gender (in)equality.

– They received *training* themselves in order to be aware, build up some expertise and be able not only to detect action domains within their own faculty or service, but also to *install good practices and opportunities therein*.

– Every year their functioning as a Mainstreaming Promoter *is evaluated* by their dean or head of service.

Good Practice

In the *University of Utrecht* a similar network is active. Within the decentralised faculties and administrative services a duo of an *academic leader* and a *personnel employee* is appointed. The academic leader is responsible for emancipation activities in the faculty or service, the personnel employee is more like an initiator and an ombudsperson who keeps an eye on the ongoing process towards more equal opportunities.[61]

As the above good practice examples illustrate, specific mechanisms for the allocation of responsibilities can best be embedded when setting up networks and activate participatory mechanisms. Thus creating *ownership* and *accountability* will definitely increase the commitment of everyone involved and contributes to the sustainability of the gender mainstreaming policy. *Ownership* is about creating opportunities for actors to achieve specific results concerning the gender mainstreaming agenda and in this way making these actors proud of their achievements. Working with systems of *accountability* has a twofold effect. *First*, the people involved are given the opportunity to integrate their mainstreaming tasks and responsibilities in the development of their personal academic career. *Second*, the risk is removed that gender mainstreaming policies are implemented in such a way that everyone is involved but no one carries responsibilities and no results are produced.

Tools for creating *responsibility* and *accountability* are[62]:

1. *On a very basic level make sure organisational structures provide an answer to the following questions:*
   - does the university provide *guidelines and codes of conduct* concerning equal opportunities?
   - who is *responsib*le for equal opportunities in the university and on its different levels of de-centralisation (e.g. in the faculties, in the University Board)?
   - who is the overall responsible actor or body that *co-ordinates* the gender mainstreaming approach?
   - is there a *dedicated group of people* with responsibility on the subject (e.g. formal or informal networks, etc)?
   - is working towards more gender equality *valued* in some way in your university?

2. *Integration of responsibilities and tasks concerning the execution of gender mainstreaming programmes in the evaluation and promotion procedures for academics, and this to different extents:*
   - start with adding gender mainstreaming responsibilities to your own curriculum vitae.
   - valuing the taking up of responsible roles in the gender mainstreaming process as a managerial performance or as a surplus value to personal academic curriculum deployment.
   - integration of gender mainstreaming responsibilities as a full criterion in the academic career development procedures.
   - setting performance targets and attaching financial bonuses for academic leaders, research units and other university services according to their progress made on the matter of gender equality.

Good Practice

Exemplary in this respect is a *Swedish university policy programme* that encloses among other measures the following elements:
- Targets were implemented for the appointment of women professors. Universities not attaining these set targets, face financial consequences
- Allocation of extra professorships in research institutes and universities where the appointments had taken place, financed by the ministry.
- Universities and faculties developing gender friendly and effective appointment policies got extra assistants and professorships.
- University Boards and various committees and commissions within universities have to consist of a minimum of 30% women; for Research Councils the target is set on 40% women.[63]

2. Developing gender mainstreaming *policy and strategic plans*

Management of the different core-activities of universities requires policy plans and strategic planning over one or more years. Deploying an overview of policies and strategies concerning the gender mainstreaming process is a very effective tool for guaranteeing realistic implementation.

How can a policy plan be developed?

1. The first step entails an overview of existing equal opportunities structures or responsible persons in the organisation. A short, but complete report on their mission, their responsibilities, their partnerships, their budgets, their personnel composition, their organigram and their realisations.

2. If there are no formal equal opportunity bodies or policy initiatives in your university, try to map all voluntary initiatives and people involved. Make a report on their efforts and effects, hereby stressing the need for organisational embedding and structural support.

3. Put together a detailed overview of the future planning of gender mainstreaming activities:
   - What are the topics to be handled by gender mainstreaming policies (based on research findings, SWOT-analyses[64], personnel statistics, etc.)?
   - What are the planned measures and actions?

- *description of the type of action (research, human resources measure, consultancy, etc.)*
- *goals, targets and results of these measures and actions*
- *time tables for each of these measures/actions (short term 1-2 years: detailed planning in time, long term 3-5 years: detailed planning in time)*
- *responsible persons for the deployment of these actions and measures*
- *budget of these measures (in terms of the amount of money needed / in terms of the different financial sources available)*
- *personnel planning*

4. Negotiate your plan, topic by topic and more important with the right people!

3. Developing effective *organisational infrastructures* in research, education and scientific services

Focusing on the supportive institutional framework is an essential tool within the protocol of implementation and organisation. In fact, mainstreaming requires the deployment of *new equality structures* and *the revision of existing equality promoting actions.*[65]

Infrastructures that promote gender equality can be designed to support and accompany the academic organisation *as a whole*. Hereby focusing on the transforming and opening up of academic systems and procedures in order to accommodate both men and women. Other supportive infrastructures are designed to bring on solutions for inefficiencies caused by gender-specific disparities *in one of the core activities* of universities.

Other possible measures that support gender mainstreaming implementation and organisation in universities are[66]:
- appointment of gender equality officers or other responsible persons with gender mainstreaming expertise;
- installing gender equality policies centres, committees or bodies, again with expertise on gender mainstreaming;
- installing channels of communication, with open access to everyone in the university, concerning the gender mainstreaming policy and bodies in the academia (e.g. construction of web-site, etc);
- installing open and gender-neutral procedures for harassment and bullying;
- installing well-published and gender-neutral procedures for handling discipline and grievances;
- creating opportunities and installing specific measures for ameliora-

tion of the work-life balance, without gender related effects (e.g. working part-time cannot compromise future promotion steps).

4. Mapping, using and achieving *gender expertise* inside and outside the organisation

Implementing gender mainstreaming in the university structures is to be done by academic leaders already active in the organisation and on different organisational levels. These actors in different study and policy domains can best be offered opportunities to learn about gender.

The best ways for gaining information about the working of gender in knowledge-organisations are:

- identifying and using *gender expertise in your university*. Hereby, contacts and co-operation with departments like gender studies or women studies can offer valuable insights and learning possibilities;
- organising *training* for key-actors in the gender mainstreaming process (e.g. actors involved in human resources departments). Practices show that experts from outside the own university can best offer gender training;
- in some policy domains, *learning instruments* are developed. The SMART-Instrument, for example, was developed for accompanying officials in personnel management in public offices. SMART stands for *Simple Method to Assess the Relevance of policies To gender*. The instrument offers a new perspective on personnel management by outlining direct and indirect effects of specific policies on the gender relations in the organisation. SMART is an easy-to-use instrument.[67]
- *networking*, in and outside the university;
- *benchmarking*. Looking at similar organisations and how they organise equal opportunities policies.

Good Practice

The internal network of *Mainstreaming Promoters (see above) of the University of Leuven* does not consist of gender mainstreaming specialists. They are male and female academics and administrators at different stages of their careers. To meet their need for knowledge and learning about gender and its mechanisms, they received a full day of gender training. This training was offered by an external training and consultancy bureau.[68]

4. Do's and Don'ts

- Implementing gender mainstreaming in your university is *not free of costs* for the organisation. The financial effect is to be calculated and budgeted. In the long run your financial efforts will be rewarded. The cost of not mainstreaming gender equality is incalculable!
- Try to explain the *temporary necessity of some positive action measures*, focusing merely on women's disadvantaged position in the different domains of academic life. Some stimulating programmes for women only, are welcome, supportive, but complementary. They are merely kick-starters, not the engine of the gender mainstreaming strategy!
- When involving all the stakeholders, make sure you get your *male colleagues* convinced of the benefits of a gender mainstreaming strategy. Point out the fact that gender mainstreaming is about guaranteeing equal opportunities for both sexes, not just for women.
- As gender mainstreaming is a *long-term process*, the overall result is not to be expected in a short time. It is a good idea though, when designing your policy plan, to aim for some quick-wins on a short-term basis. In that way, you keep people interested and motivated.

2.3.3 Building Awareness & Ownership

1. Awareness & ownership: what's their use?

Building awareness and ownership means to assure a basic level of understanding and expertise on the subject of gender, and a certain level of responsibility to change existing gender relations.

However, not all policy makers, managers and academic leaders are experts in the area of gender and diversity. If you want them to incorporate gender issues in their products and practices, you have to make sure that they have at least a basic level of *training and expertise* to hand. Just like you would never assign people to budgeting without any training or expertise, you cannot expect them to perform gender mainstreaming without any awareness building programmes, training, tool-kits, or guidelines.

Another necessary step if you want gender mainstreaming to be successful is to *build ownership*. Not only should people be conscious of the working of gender as a social ordination mechanism, but they should also consider it their task and responsibility to resolve potential gender discriminatory effects. All the way through the organisation, relevant actors have to be ready to initiate, implement, and co-ordinate the gender mainstreaming process. In Chapter One you can find many arguments, which you can use to convince academic leaders, managers, and policy makers that gender mainstreaming is not only in the organisation's interest, but also in their own. Conviction alone though is not enough. No matter how eager people are for change, their initiatives will inevitably fail if they do not have sufficient time, means, and competence to actually realise their ideas (see above § Implementation and Organisation).

2. Why building gender awareness and ownership?

Many organisations expect people to do mainstreaming 'without so much as a back of an envelope's training'.[69] Apparently, they assume that anyone is capable to trace gender biases. This assumption is easily made, since gender stereotypes are so much part of our daily lives. Who doesn't know the stereotype that women are more caring, sensitive and co-operative, whereas men are more self-supportive, rational and competitive? The difficulty of gender biases is that most of them are hard to trace by an untrained eye exactly *because* we are continuously exposed to them. Gender stereotypes are affirmed and reproduced by all kinds of 'vehicles' in daily life such as papers, magazines, adverts, movies and television, but also by education, socialisation, family relations and contacts in public and private life. Often, we are not even aware that we are reproducing them in our own behaviour.

The following example illustrates that norms and values about what is perceived as 'masculine' and 'feminine', can cause serious dilemmas for women operating in 'masculine' cultures.

Illustration

In 1999, the Dutch professor in labour and organisational psychology A. Fischer conducted a study on the norms, values and behaviour concerning *leadership in the Dutch ministry of agriculture*.[70] The study, based on an inquiry among 169 randomly selected respondents, showed that women at the top more often feel themselves to be judged as 'too hard' if they behave the same as their male colleagues. The behavioural repertoire of women in top positions appears to be limited by two inter-acting mechanisms: on the one hand, they risk disapproval if they break with the implicit norm that women are more gentle and social than men, whereas on the other hand, their behaviour is more likely to be stamped as 'soft' if they do conform with the stereotype manners.

Fisher describes this ambiguity in the valuation and interpretation of women's behaviour as a '*paradox of emotions*'. Women are praised for their social and communicative competence, but if they overtly show emotional feelings, they are judged to be less suitable for the top.[71]

Gender stereotypes not only fix women and men in specific roles and positions which do not automatically fit their needs, talents and ambitions. They also reflect *patterns of power*. Gender codes are based on dualism (e.g. mind versus body, intuition versus rational analysis, co-operation versus competition) in which the 'male' is structurally raised as the norm and 'female' characteristics are defined as a negation or deriva-tion of the male norm or are perceived as inferior.[72] The public sphere, for example, traditionally seen as the domain of men, is generally perceived as more important than the private sphere, which has been associated with women for ages.

This *hierarchical order* strengthens the need for breaching gender mecha-nisms. Social injustice is involved, since 'feminine' and 'masculine' roles and positions are not equally valued, also *in the material sense* (e.g. pay grading systems). In the context of universities there is the skewed distri-bution of research grants over the different disciplines. Male-dominated areas like Science and Technology are prioritised, mostly at the cost of areas in which women are relatively well-represented.[73] It is exactly this hierarchy that partly hinders the transformation of traditional gender patterns.

3. Awareness building tools

Awareness building tools are designed to make people conscious of existing distinctions between the sexes as described above. They explain the working of gender as an organising mechanism, and show how gender stereotypes affect the opportunities and position of women and men. You can optimise their effectiveness by explicitly referring to practices and figures derived from your own organisation.

To increase people's gender awareness *Deloitte & Touche* organised a series of workshops for all management professionals in its US offices, including the board of directors, the management committee, and the managing partners.

Deloitte & Touche Best Practice

"I'm sure I wasn't the only partner calculating in my head the lost revenue represented by two days'worth of billable hours, multiplied by 5,000 – not to mention the $8 million cost of the workshops themselves. I was dead wrong. *The workshops were a turning point, a pivotal event in the life of the firm.* Through discussions, videos and case studies, we began to take a hard look at how gender attitudes affected the environment at Deloitte. It wasn't enough to hear the problems in the abstract; we had to see them face to face. Sitting across a table from a respected colleague and hearing her say 'Why did you make that assumption about women? It's just not true', I, like many others, began to change".[74] [...]

"*Case studies were useful for bringing out and examining subtle differences in expectations.* Drawing on scripts provided by outside facilitators, people in the workshops would break into groups, discuss cases, and share solutions with the full group. A typical scenario would have partners evaluating two promising young professionals, a woman and a man with identical skills. Of the woman, a partner would say, 'She's really good, she gives 100%. But I just don't see her interacting with a CFO. She's not as polished as some. Her presentation skills could be stronger.' The conversation about the man would vary slightly, but significantly: 'He's good. He and I are going to take a CFO golfing next week. I know he can grow into it; he has tremendous potential.' Beginning with these subtle variations in *language*, careers could go in very different directions."[75] [...]

"Scenarios like these lent realism to the workshop discussions, and hard-hitting dialogue often ensued. One partner was jolted into thinking about an outing he was going to attend, an annual "guys' weekend" with partners from the Atlanta office and many of their clients. It was very popular, and there were never any women. It hadn't occurred to him to ask why. *He figured* 'no woman would want to go to a golf outing where you smoke cigars and drink beer and tell lies'. But the women in the session were quick to say that by not being there, they were frozen out of *informal networks where important information was shared* and a sense of belonging built. Today women are routinely included in such outings. *Work assignments* got a lot of attention in the workshops. Everyone knew that high-profile, high-revenue assignments were the key to advancement in the firm. Careers were made on big clients, you grew up on the Microsoft engagement, the Chrysler engagement. But the process of assigning these plum accounts was largely unexamined. Too often, women were passed over for certain assignments because male partners made assumptions about what they wanted: 'I wouldn't put her on that kind of company because it's a tough manufacturing environment', or 'That client is difficult to deal with'. Even more common, 'Travel puts too much pressure on women' or 'Her husband won't go along with relocating'. *Usually, we weren't even conscious of making such assumptions, but the workshops brought them front and center.* The workshops also highlighted one of the worst aspects of these hidden assumptions: *they were self-fulfilling.* Say a partner gets a big new client and asks the assignment director to put together a team, adding, 'Continuity is very important on this engagement'. The assignment director knows that women turn over more rapidly than men and has the numbers to prove it. So the thinking goes, 'If I put a woman on this account, the partner will be all over me – and that's who evaluates me.' In the end, John gets to work on the big account and Jane works 'somewhere else'. After a while, Jane says, 'I'm not going to get anywhere here. I'm never going to get the big opportunities', so she leaves. And the assignment director says, 'I knew it.' The task force realised the workshops were risky; the firm was opening a can of worms and couldn't control the results. Indeed, a few of the workshops flopped, disintegrating into a painful mixture of bitterness and scepticism. [...] *But ultimately the workshops converted a critical mass of Deloitte's leaders. The message was out: don't make assumptions about what women do or don't want. Ask them.*"[76]

Awareness building tools can be divided into *three categories*. Below, some examples of tools in each of the three categories are listed. Each of them reflects a form of awareness that is indispensable for successful gender mainstreaming. Hence, if you want to build awareness in your organisation, your programmes will be most effective if they combine elements of all three categories.

1. Educational techniques and instruments

This category of awareness building tools consists of instruments designed to increase the general gender expertise of academic leaders, managers and policy makers. These tools enable people to uncover gender biases in seemingly neutral norms, practices and procedures.

* Training trajectories
* Workshops
* Manuals
* Tool-kits
* Guidelines

2. Collection and dissemination of facts and figures inside the organisation

The second category of tools is explicitly aimed at the situation in your organisation. They help you to measure the status quo, monitor progress and assess the gender impact of measures and practices.

* Measurement & monitoring
* Systematic publication of sex-segregated data in management information reports and annual report
* Gender-impact assessments
* Dissemination of gender research results

3. Consultation and participation

The last set of instruments consists of consultation and participation tools designed to assist people to promote gender diversity by exchanging experiences and good practices, and promoting optimal utilisation of existing gender expertise in and outside the organisation.

* Consultancy of gender experts
* Expertise centres
* Networks
* Databases
* Digital forums: websites, e-mail discussion lists, etc
* Panels of experts or 'thinking-tanks'
* Working groups
* Committees
* Hearings

Good Practice

A good practice example of the first category of awareness building tools is the *Centre of Excellence Women and Science (CEWS)* started up in september 2000 at *Bonn University.* This Centre which is funded by the Federal Ministry for Education and Research (*Bundesministerium für Bildung und Forschung*) "is to become a national co-ordination and information centre and an advisory office with an international dimension for scientific and political organisations and institutions dealing with gender equity in science and research as well as for women's affairs and equal rights commissioners and women researchers in Germany and abroad.[77]"

www.cews.uni-bonn.de

Good Practice

The Athena Project, UK

The Athena Project[78] is a UK wide initiative, developed out of the Committee of Vice Chancellors and Pricipals ' (CVCP) Commission on University Career Opportunity's agenda to remove barriers to discrimination to women in higher education and to significantly increase the number of women in top posts by 2007.

The Athena Project aims at:
- drawing on existing good human resource practice within and outside higher education;
- encouraging and supporting the development of good practice;
- disseminating learning and good practice to Higher Education Institutes;
- and contributing to and responding to external initiatives on women in Science, Engineering and Technology (SET).

During the year 2000 several networks were launched within the Athena Project. These Athena networks are called 'Local Academic Women's Networks' (LAWNs) and programme the following activities:
- seminar programmes showcasing women academics;
- workplace shadowing;
- discussion seminars for (potential) returners / part-timers / job sharers;
- research seminars;
- meetings to identify / generate cross-disciplinary research opportunities;
- seminars for women undergraduate and graduate students;
- conferences for women in the early years of their academic careers;
- workshops on writing successful research grant proposals.

www.athena.ic.ac.uk

4. Ownership Building Tools

Ownership building tools are tools designed to stimulate people to take gender mainstreaming seriously and do something about it. Successful ownership building will only happen if certain prerequiqites are fulfilled. These conditions are *the assignment of a formal responsibility, basic training, sufficient resources and gender awareness*. The top of the organisation has an important role in ownership building. *Academic leaders and managers* can stress the seriousness of the matter by acting as pioneers in recruiting and promoting women, transforming discriminatory practices and actively carrying out the conviction that gender equality is a basic prerequisite for promoting excellence. Apart from this, *setting targets and organising public pressure*, thus causing a healthy level of competitiveness, may help you to build ownership. But probably the most effective way to stimulate ownership is systematically reviewing – and rewarding or sanctioning – people's efforts and results. In this process it is important to *make your efforts towards gender mainstreaming visible and transparent*.

In *Deloitte & Touche*, the top succeeded to build ownership by overtly letting the world watch its efforts. It held a press conference to launch the Women's Initiative, and named an external advisory council, consisting of business leaders with expertise in the area of women in the workplace, chaired by Lynn Martin, former U.S. Secretary of Labour.

Deloitte & Touche Best Practice

"Besides reviewing the Initiative's progress, the council brought visibility to the effort. As the task force realized, going public would put healthy pressure on the partners to commit to change and deliver results. And that's what happened, particularly with slow-moving offices in the organization. Local managers received prodding comments from their associates like, 'I read in the Wall Street Journal that we're doing this major initiative, but I don't see big change in our office'. The council has held the firm's feet to the fire in a variety of ways: an annual report on thelinitiative; periodic voicemail-updates from Lynn Martin to the entire firm; and full-day meetings of the council with the firm's senior executives. The council defines the challenges we still face, and it lets senior management know they're not off the hook."[79]

1. Integration of gender equality criteria in assessment procedures

These ownership building tools totally harmonise with the mainstreaming strategy. Their effectiveness is increased when combined with positive or negative sanctioning.

- Setting concrete gender mainstreaming targets
- Integrating these targets in:
  - *performance-based financing to universities, research funding, conferences, etcetera;*
  - *individual performance reviews of staff members, especially staff members who are formally responsible for implementing gender mainstreaming;*
  - *quality management models (see Chapter Three)*

2. Positive incentives

These measures have no transforming capacity as such. They are merely 'add-on' tools that support the gender mainstreaming process.

- Bonuses
- Prizes
- Labels and hallmarks

3. Competitiveness and public pressure

Publicity gives visibility to the gender mainstreaming policies. Thus focusing on the success, or indeed failure, of responsible actors.

- Regular publication of results inside and outside the organisation
- Establishing (external) revision and advisory committees
- Informing relevant public media about initiatives and results

Good Practice

Total E-Quality Science Award

The *German Federal Government* supports ownership building in universities by positive incentives as well as restrictive sanctions. *The Total E-quality Science Award* is a good example of such a positive incentive.

This award is intended to motivate universities and research institutions to integrate innovative forms of equality into their organisation processes.

It allows for the comparison of different programmes aimed at the promotion of equal opportunities at universities and research institutes. With the help of a special measurement tool, based on a check list, universities can *self-assess* their position with respect to the promotion of equal opportunities and *compare themselves* to other universities and institutions that apply for the total e-quality science award. This is meant as an incentive for the universities and research institutions to improve their equal opportunity policies.

www.Total-E-Quality-Science.de

Good Practice

Financing of universities based on performance.[80]

The German concept of financing universities, performance-based means that the progress made in universities towards establishing equal opportunities for women and men is *one of the criteria for the funding of universities*. Other criteria are the universities' achievements with respect to research and education and the promotion of young scientists.[81]

In North Rhine-Westphalia (NRW) for example, progress made towards equal opportunities for women and men is taken into account with respect to the financing of universities by the Ministry of Education, Science and Research.[82] In addition it serves as a criterion in the internal distribution of funding at universities.

Regarding the internal distribution of funding, the law[83] specifies that the universities' progress is to be measured with respect to the following:
- the participation of women in innovative developments and projects
- the share of women among academic personnel and professors
- the increase of the share of female students, particularly in the natural sciences, engineering and medicine.

The implementation of the new law at the *University of Bonn* means that in 2001 for the first time DM 200,000 were taken from the university budget and distributed according to the progress made towards equal opportunities for men and women. Of this sum, DM 150,000 have been distributed to departmental units based on the progress they have made. Their progress is measured by examining the share of female professors, the share of women having finished their habilitation and the share of women having finished their dissertation. The remaining DM 50,000 are used for the funding of special projects aiming at the promotion of women that have applied for by the departments. Examples include projects aimed at increasing the participation of women in natural sciences and engineering, mentoring projects and summer courses for female high school students.

5. Do's and don'ts

1. Awareness building tools are most effective if they *directly confront people* with their own behaviour and attitude:
   - to illustrate the working of gender mechanisms, *use near and recognisable examples*, rather than abstract theories;
   - stimulate people to *reflect* on their own assumptions and behaviour, rather than on other's.

2. Create ownership by arguing that *gender mainstreaming is good for everyone:*
   - stress that gender relations *limit the behavioural repertoire of both sexes*: they fix women and men in roles that do not necessary fit their personality and ambitions;
   - do not accuse or victimise anyone, but make clear what's the *impact* of gender biases and unverified assumptions for women and men;
   - don't make emotional appeals, but argue why investments are necessary by *documenting the costs of doing nothing*: female scientists' high turnover rates, the low percentage of female students in undersubscribed science and technology areas, the imminent lack of well-qualified scientific personnel, etc.

3. Never think you're ready:
   - gender mainstreaming is an *on-going process*. The job isn't done by organising one workshop, prize or expertise centre. Gender awareness and ownership have to be built by a constant flow of mutually attuned incentives;
   - never stick to awareness building alone, be sure to provide *incentives and sufficient means and instruments* for people to do something with the knowledge acquired;
   - *attune* awareness and ownership building schemes to other instruments applied in the process of gender mainstreaming. Statistical measurements and gender impact assessments provide data and insights which are directly relevant to consciousness and ownership building, and vice versa.
   - *prevent duplication and re-invention of the wheel,* by facilitating the exchange of ideas and good practices, e.g. by establishing an expertise centre or co-ordinative network.

Deloitte & Touche Best Practice

Douglas M. McCracken finishes his article about the firm's Women's Initiative by stating that it has generated greater creativity, faster growth, and far greater performance for the clients, but that there are still plenty of challenges.

"The changes at Deloitte are by no means complete. For many years, women have made up one-third to one-half of Deloitte's recruits, so we need to make sure the percentage of women partners and directors rises well above 14%. And we face new challenges. Now that more women are becoming partners, how can we make sure they continue to develop and advance into positions of leadership?"[84] [...]

"Still, we have transformed our work environment, even in the smallest details. When a visiting speaker – even a client – cracks a joke at women's expense, none of us laughs, not even politely. One partner turned down an invitation to join a premier lunch club in Manhattan when he learned it excluded women. And we've opened our eyes to differences in style that go beyond gender to include culture. For example, on a recent client engagement, the project manager described an Asian consultant on his team as "shy" and therefore not ready to take on more responsibility. But another partner pushed the project manager for details and suggested that consultants could still be successful, even if they didn't "command a room" or raise their voices when speaking in meetings."[85]

2.3.4 Gender Proofing and Evaluation

1. Do you know the gender impact of your products and practices?

Gender proofing means critically analysing organisational structures, policy procedures, products, concepts and values in order to eliminate any potential discriminatory effects and promote gender diversity.

Gender codes – norms and values about women and men and how they should behave in public and private life – are embedded in all kinds of structures and practices by which society is shaped. Although gender codes have an impact on both women and men, in the academic context, women are more forcefully confronted with them, since traditionally universities were primarily the domain of men. Until the beginning of the

20th century, women were not even admitted to most West European universities, for no other reason than their biological sex. Due to this historical sex-segregation, women had little share in shaping current practices and procedures in the academic world, or the content of scientific knowledge itself. The consequences of these gendered patterns of segregation are still perceptible today. Many regulations, structures and procedures, but also research issues and curriculum designs are implicitly based on male norms and values to which women are less likely to conform, less willing to conform or to which it is *assumed* that they do not conform.

Gender proofing stimulates you to wonder how science and its institutions would have looked if women and men had been equally involved in the construction of the academic world right from their origin. Would the image of the distracted professor, performing abstract research in his ivory tower ever have developed if all professors had their daily share in time-consuming, down-to earth matters like the care of infirm parents, preparing food or cleaning dirty diapers? Wouldn't academic disciplines have evolved around different questions if women had been involved in their construction right from the start? By deconstructing all kinds of gender-biases in the academic system, gender proofing aims to analyse and transform, step by step, the everyday reality of universities. Hence, it can be seen as the quintessence of gender mainstreaming.

2. Why gender proofing?

Throughout their academic careers women are faced with barriers that are ingrained in seemingly neutral rules and procedures by which the production of science is organised. Output norms and review procedures, for instance, which are based on the number of publications and citations are indirectly discriminative to women, since women are more often involved in part-time jobs and have career breaks (e.g. pregnancy leave). Hence, women as a group are less likely to meet these criteria than their male colleagues.[86]

Similar discriminatory effects have been detected in procedures for the distribution of research grants[87], wages[88], and access to research facilities and databases[89]. Also less tangible matters, like the organisational culture[90], or informal networking practices[91], have proven to be troubling to female scientists. These subtle forms of discrimination might be hardly alarming at first sight, but each scientific career is based on many of these small decisions. A study at the Massachusetts Institute of Technology has illustrated, that the accumulation of these small disadvantages have a large impact on the development of women careers on the long term.[92] *Gender proofing helps you to uncover both overt and subtle gender biases in the scientific system and identify ways to transform them.*

Gender proofing is not exclusively aimed to removing barriers for women, but enlarges the behavioural repertoire of both sexes to work and live according to their own needs and demands. Recent labour market studies show that a growing number of young male employees prefer to work part-time, and wishes to share bread-winning and caring responsibilities with their partners.[93] The fact that in many academic institutes, the conditions for promotion are still in favour of scientists who are able to dedicate at least 40 hours a week fully to research and education is not only a burden to women careers but diminishes the attractiveness of a career in science to a broad range of people, since it neglects the need for being treated as a whole person.

The changes that were carried through in *Deloitte & Touche* in the context of the Women's Initiative, eventually appeared to benefit the company as a whole.

Deloitte & Touche Best Practice

"Moving toward equality in career development was fundamental. But as people began to discuss gender issues in workshops, meetings, and hallways, what started out as a program for women soon began to affect our overall corporate culture. [...] We discovered that work-life balance was important to everyone. On paper, we had always allowed temporary, flexible work arrangements, but people believed (rightly, at the time) that working fewer hours could doom an otherwise promising career. In 1993, only a few hundred people were taking advantage of the policy. So now we said that opting for flexible work wouldn't hinder advancement in the firm, though it might stretch out the time required for promotion. Use of these arrangements became one more benchmark of an office's progress with the initiative. And when a woman was admitted to the partnership in 1995 while on a flexible work arrangement, people really began to get the message. By 1999 more than 30 people on flexible work arrangements had made partner, and in that year, the total number of people on flexible work schedules had doubled to 800. We also re-examined the schedule that all of us work, especially within the consulting practice. A grinding travel schedule had long been an accepted part of the macho consultant's culture. Typically, a consultant was away from home five days a week, for up to 18 months at a time. In 1996, we started a new schedule, dubbed the 3-4-5 program. Consultants working on out-of-town projects were to be away from home three nights a week, at the client site four days a week, and in their local Deloitte offices on the fifth day. [...] In fact, many of us were concerned initially that the program would compromise client service. But most clients embraced our new program. It turned out that employees from the client's regional offices were exhausted, too, by travelling to meet Deloitte's team at their home offices all week long. One day each week without the Deloitte consultants at their sites was a relief, not an inconvenience! By breaking the collective silence about the personal price everyone was paying, we made everyone happier. [...] As a result of these and other changes, we've transformed our culture into one in which people are comfortable talking about aspects of their personal lives, going well beyond client assignments and career development. Teams are getting requests like 'I want to talk to my kids every night at 7:00 [...]' or 'I'd really like to go to the gym in the morning, so can we start our meetings at 8:30 instead of 7:30?' This more open environment not only helps us keep our rising stars but also makes us more creative in a variety of areas."[94]

3. Gender proofing and evaluation tools

The most familiar tools for gender proofing are *gender impact assessments*. Gender impact assessments are analytical tools, designed to check whether or not specific practices affect women and men differently, with a view to adapting them to make sure that potential gender biases are eliminated. This adaptation goes further than simply replacing sex-specific words like 'women' and 'men' by 'gender neutral' terms like people or human beings: even if women and men are addressed equally, measures can affect them differently because of the diverging roles and qualities that are attributed to women and men in society. Gender impact assessments explicitly take into account such differences, while guarding from reproducing or affirming current gender stereotypes.

Gender impact assessments can be applied to all kinds of practices, varying from selection and recruitment procedures, financial resources and quality control systems, to the organisation's culture and the content of research and educational programmes. Depending on the kind of practices analysed they can take many forms. Several standardised tools have been developed to assist policy and decision makers in evaluating their own practices, but most gender impact assessments have a more 'ad hoc' character.

In the explanation of tools below, a distinction is made between *three areas of analysis*, which are specifically relevant in the academic context. These three areas – policy making, research and education, and organisational culture – are not exhaustive. Together, however, they provide an impression of the broad range of issues that could be investigated if you want to gender proof your organisation's products and practices.

1. Gender proofing and evaluating policy making

In policy making, gender proofing means incorporating gender diversity as an integral issue in all stadia of the policy process: *planning, decision making, implementation and evaluation afterwards*.[95] When your organisation is developing new policy lines and procedures it has an excellent chance to integrate gender issues right from the start into all phases of the policy making process. However, gender impact assessments can also very well used to gender proof existing policy practices. In each phase of the policy making process different kinds of questions are relevant. The following framework can be used as a *checklist* for identifying relevant questions:

■ *Planning and prepatory phase:*

In this phase gender impact assessments are useful for putting women's issues and perspectives on the political agenda and for identifying the way in which traditional gender codes affect the policy area. Relevant questions are:

To what extent is gender diversity incorporated into:
• the articulation and definition of problems and challenges?
• the process of valuing their scope, urgency and priority?
• the identification of targets groups?
• the identification of goals and targets?

■ *Decision making:*

In the decision making process gender proofing is important to ensure that women's needs and values are equally considered and weighed to these of men. Relevant questions are:

To what extent is gender diversity incorporated into the process of

deciding, namely
- which of the identified problems will be addressed?
- which strategies will be pursued to solve them?
- which means will be attributed to each of the issues addressed?
- which measures and instruments will be implemented to achieve the identified goals?

■ *Implementation:*

Gender impact assessments in the implementation process are relevant to guarantee that gender issues will be taken into account in the day-to-day reality. Even if gender diversity is incorporated in the official policy goals several steps are necessary to translate them into actions. Relevant questions are:

To what extent is gender diversity incorporated in:
- the operation of policy plans?
- the process of translating them into concrete actions?
- the execution of policy measures, instruments and actions?

■ *Evaluation afterwards:*

Finally, gender proofing instruments can be used to evaluate the actual effect of policy measures on gender relations. The results of this evaluation can be used to adjust existing policy measures and develop new strategic policy lines if necessary. Relevant questions are:

What is the impact of policy measures on:
- equal opportunities and the representation of men and women?
- Images and stereotypes with respect to gender?

All kinds of policy practices in academic organisations can be analysed as described above. *The policy area that has probably been most extensively investigated during the past decades is the recruitment and selection of academic personnel.*

Illustration

Exemplary questions for a gender impact assessment in this area are provided by a detailed study of *five controversial scientific appointments at the University of Amsterdam*, conducted in charge of the *Dutch Ministry of Social Affairs.*[96] The study didn't accept the promotion committees' arguments that the quality of the candidates was the decisive factor, but critically analysed the criteria used to measure their quality. These criteria appeared to be not at all fixed. In all but one procedures the candidates' qualifications were compared on the base of several competences, but during the selection processes the weight attached to these competences was (re)ordered at will, implicitly affirming existing preferences. Each time, one specific competence, like research qualifications, or managerial competences, was raised to the norm, to which the other candidates were compared. Typically enough, this was always the outstanding competence of a male candidate. Competences in which the female candidates excelled were subordinated to the practice of selecting a candidate, despite the fact that the university formally adhered to a progressive affirmative action policy.

Relevant questions to assess the gender impact of *selection procedures* are: who decides, on the basis of which criteria and by which procedures are the competences of candidates tested, and how does this affect the chances of male and female candidates?

Arbitrariness in selection procedures doesn't serve your organisation's interests. Fairness in selection can be increased by clearly mapping the most urgently needed competences in advance, putting them in a commonly agreed order of preference, and setting up strict procedures by which all candidates are tested. By doing so, you will improve the quality of judgement, because the chance is enhanced that the best applicant is selected, irrespective of gender or other potential biases.

Likewise, all kinds of policy practices in your organisation can be gender proofed, ranging from the distribution of financial resources to the interior architecture of university buildings.

A few *examples* of similar questions in *other policy areas* are:
- *student services*: are the needs and interests of women and men equally considered and weighed in the services your organisation offers to students (e.g. facilities in sports, information and advice, international exchange programmes, measures to prevent sexual harassment)?
- *performance reviews and monitoring procedures:* are gender equality criteria systematically incorporated in performance reviews and monitoring procedures, as a feature of quality and a precondition for fostering excellence in research, education and social involvement?
- *labour conditions:* do the labour conditions of your organisation respect heterogeneous roles, aspirations, and abilities (e.g. concerning the work-life balance or the principle of life-long learning)?

- *human resources management*: which principles and criteria underpin your organisation's procedures for recruitment, selection, promotion, and competence development? Do they promote a balanced influx, mobility and exit of women and men in all functions? (see: Chapter Three, § People Management)

Illustration

The *Emancipatie Effect Rapportage* (EER), literally translated 'Emancipation Effect Report'[97], is a standardised Dutch tool for the evaluation of regular policy measures in the first stage of the policy making process: *the planning and preparatory phase*. The EER, designed by the scientists M. Verloo and C. Roggeband[98] to assess the gender impact of new strategic courses and policy lines consists of *eight steps*:

1. Do we need a gender impact analysis – does the policy area in which we are operating involve gender relations and/or gender inequalities?
2. Describe the policy proposal to be analysed.
3. Describe present differences between women and men in this policy area.
4. Describe how differences between women and men in this policy area would develop without policy intervention.
5. Analyse the (underlying) assumptions of the policy proposal as described in step 2 concerning problem definition, proposed solution, cause-effect relations, means-end relations.
6. Check whether the policy proposal takes into account sex differences, inequalities in resources, and current gender codes: are policy makers aware that their proposal has a potential gender impact?
7. Describe how the policy proposal could affect current gender relations: does it promote heterogeneity and autonomy of the sexes.
8. Conclusion, based on step 7 compared to step 4: does the policy proposal improve, stabilise or worsen the situation, compared to the situation as expected without policy intervention?

In the Netherlands, the EER has been applied by a broad range of actors (e.g. the national government) in such varied areas as the election system, heritage legislation, higher education, and ICT in education. It has proven to be a useful instrument to analyse how gender mechanisms affect specific policy areas and measures, and vice versa. It is especially valuable as a step-by-step guide for in-depth policy analysis. Evaluation has shown that the instrument is most effective if conducted by external (gender) experts, and if implemented in an early phase of the policy process, so that the analysed policy plans can still be adjusted before proposing them to the decision makers.[99] *Various descriptions and evaluations of the EER-protocol are available in English.*[100]

2. Gender proofing and evaluating research and education

Gender impact assessments cannot only be applied to academic policy making, but can also be used as to *the content of research and education*. Three potential entrances for a gender impact assessment in *research* are the *issues* that are studied, the *language* that is used, and the *methods* that are applied.[101]

With respect to the *research issues*, you could investigate how priorities are set. How are choices made about what we want to know,and what we choose not to know? For whom is the investigated problem relevant? Whose interests are served by the knowledge that is build?

With respect to *language* used in scientific research, you can use gender impact assessments to uncover gender biases and stereotypes embedded in seemingly innocent practices. These practices could vary from using 'men' as an inclusive term that supposedly covers women as well, to outright sexist metaphors. Terminology determines the direction of scientific practice, the questions asked, the results obtained and the interpretations deduced.

A relevant issue of analysis concerning research *methods* is the population chosen for study. Are women and men equally represented, and if not, what is the reason behind this choice? Another methodological choice you could investigate by a gender impact assessment are the criteria that are used to determine what needs explanation and what counts as evidence.

Illustration

The *Research and Resources Unit* of the GB *Equal Opportunities Commission* developed a useful *Checklist for gender proofing research*[102] in which the following items are highlighted:
- *the meaning of gender proofing* research and its applications: building a gender dimension into all stages of a research project, which means concretely thinking about the gender implications of choices;
- *financial incentives*: funding organisations could require applicants to

demonstrate that they have built a gender dimension into their projects where appropriate;
- the problem of research projects *focusing explicitly on one gender*;
- the problem of assuming that men and women are *two homogeneous groups*;
- the necessity of including a *gender-specific analysis* in final research reports.

http://www.eoc.uk

In academic *education*, gender impact assessments could be based on analogue questions as in research. With respect to the *issues* of education, the development of the curriculum is an obvious object of analysis. Who decides what kind of knowledge students should acquire? Based on which criteria? Are these issues equally attractive for male and female students?

Concerning *language*, all study material could be analysed based on the question: to what extent do they equally address women and men, and help to reduce gender stereotypes? These questions can also be applied to the lectures and exams of individual educators.

Finally, gender impact assessments in education could focus on the *methods and technologies* applied. It might be necessary to increase the diversity of methods in order to be able to meet the individual teaching and coaching demands of male and female students effectively.

Good Practice

Action

Action is an instrument developed by the *Dutch Organisation for Women in Higher Technical Education and Positions*[103] designed for accompanying people active in the developing, conducting and evaluation of educational programmes. Action focuses on the implementation of innovative educational methods like, projectwise education and problem-based education, hereby outlining enabling conditions for women that can increase the attractiveness of advanced technology education for female students. Action entails a diagnosis-instrument, an evaluation instrument and an implementation guide.[104]

Good Practice

Gender Inclusive Curriculum

The same Dutch *Organisation for Women in Higher Technical Education and Positions* (VHTO) also participates in the Mellow-project (see: Chapter Three, § Customer Results). This as an expert organisation on the increasing women's participation in technology and technology education. Within the Mellow-Framework, VHTO is doing a project called the *Gender Inclusive Curriculum*. This pilot study aimes at investigating the ongoing educational innovations in the *Universities of Professional Education* in the Netherlands. VHTO-WiTEC Netherlands[105] is listing and describing these changes in order to evaluate them on the following aspects:
– elements that are useful for the design of a basic model for attractive technological curricula;
– elements that raise the attractiveness and learnability of technological education for female students.

http://www.vhto.nl

3. Organisational culture

The culture in an organisation is shaped by the interaction of values, opinions and social practices that affect the way in which the organisation's people function.[106] It creates patterns of expectations throughout the organisation, regarding the accepted manners towards colleagues and superiors, and the way in which activities are performed. These expectations are to a large extent decisive for the kind of employers that are valued within the organisation. They affect which people are selected and promoted, or indeed, rejected. Through this interaction of norms and practices, the culture is reproduced.

Ideally, the institutional climate functions as a binding factor in the organisation: people identify with the organisation's image and ethics, and mutually expect each other to carry out the organisation's mission and strategic purposes. But it can also have an exclusionary effect. If people do not feel comfortable with the dominant norms and practices, they might be inclined to leave the organisation. Likewise, well-qualified candidates might decide not to fulfil a vacant function if they do not like the institutional climate.[107]

Various researchers studying the relatively slow career path and quick departure of female scientists have concluded that the culture, values and customs within universities are less compatible with women's needs and values than men's. Their slow progress and premature exit are not only caused by personal factors like pregnancy or (child)care responsibilities. Organisational customs like the role of informal networking[108], norms with respect to (full-time) availability and commitment[109], and the level of support and mentorship of superiors[110], have proven to be at least as important. Gender proofing the organisational culture helps you to attract and retain talented women to your organisation.

There are various entrances to perform a gender impact assessment on your organisation's culture. One way is to examine key communications of the top and decentralised units, like the university's mission statement, the opening speech of the academic year, annual reports, codes of conduct, policy plans and information brochures: do they reflect an open-minded, innovative and well thought-out attitude towards gender and diversity? Even if the organisation formally subscribed to gender diversity, a discrepancy between theory and practice can be reflected in images and assumptions embedded in the organisation's key communications.

Another way for evaluating the organisational culture is to interview male and female scientists and/or students, asking them how they experience the institutional culture and the way in which they are approached by colleagues, superiors, and/or educators. This strategy allows you to compare the organisations' official ethics and identity with the everyday customs and practices. Inquiries based on a large and representative population could be useful to check whether women and men experience them in a different way and have different cultural preferences.

Relevant issues for such inquiries can be derived from studies, in which specific aspects of the culture of organisations have been analysed, such as:
- leadership styles[111]
- mentoring practices[112]
- current norms with respect to availability and private responsibilities[113]
- status and valuation of 'masculine' and 'feminine' values[114]
- access to and role of (informal) networks[115]
- systems of power and authority[116]
- sexual harassment and other unsolicited forms of behaviour[117]
- language and communication[118]

Illustration

In 1998, the *University of Maastricht* published a study on the way in which men and women, masculinity and femininity, were constructed in the everyday context of the university.[119] All kinds of written material were investigated, in which the university (implicitly) expressed its vision on education, research, science, and management, such as: information brochures of student services, annual reports, study manual, policy plans and faculty magazines. The analysis was not limited to textual communications, but also paid attention to images reflected in photographs and illustrations. Some promotion movies were examined as well. The aim of the analysis was to uncover the ways in which an 'invisible distinction' was made between the sexes.

Men and science appeared to be linked to each other as self-evident, whereas women, at least in texts and visual images, were to a large extent excluded from science. In communications concerning students, women were relatively well represented, but as soon as a communication dealt with research, education and management, women as a group vanished almost completely. They were most extremely under-represented in official reports and articles with respect to senior research, education and management functions. In the rare occasions that women were present on the base of their profession in science or management, invariably associations turned up with traditional female stereotypes concerning the body, motherhood, beauty or charm. Unlike their male colleagues, they were hardly ever presented as actively operating, respectable professionals.

The effect of these one-sided representations of women and men is two-fold. Women as a group are implicitly excluded, and the status quo is indirectly maintained by a vicious circle: since few senior posts in science are occupied by women, women are almost absent in communications concerning these functions, which strengthens the image of senior posts in science as 'masculine'. This image directly affects career choices of women and men, and even the judgement of selection and appointment committees on the suitability of male and female candidates for senior posts.

The report provides a broad range of recommendations on how universities can 'gender proof' their communications, such as:

- Increase the number of female editors and authors, preferably experts in the area of gender and diversity;
- Consciously search for female scientists and experts in interviews; if there aren't any female professionals, ask female students for their opinion;

- Place as many photographs of female scientists and experts in function in your communications as possible, mentioning their name, title, and function;
- Prevent traditional images of femininity: don't use pictures of nameless and functionless women as decoration, or relate them to the body, beauty, motherhood, care, or hobby. Transform these images;
- Likewise, prevent traditional images of masculinity: do not only associate men with power, authority, rationality, science, etc, but try to transform these images;
- In the presentation of names and titles, do not mention people's sex only if they are women, but refer to people's sex by using 'ms' as well as 'mr';
- In photographs, mind the position of the camera and the mise-en-scène: prevent that women are pictured from above and men from below, and record women in a working environment and/or active position;
- Be vigilant in using 'he/she', instead of only he, and be aware of comparable exclusionary linguistic mechanisms;
- Organise training programmes about effective image building and breaking traditional gender codes intended for academic leaders, information managers, editors, photographers, and other people involved in your organisation's communication and information policy.

4. Do's & don'ts

1. Do set priorities

Since gender codes run through practically all practices and procedures in your organisation, gender proofing your organisation requires an accurate setting and resetting of priorities, in a continuous process of change.

- Before performing a gender impact assessment, ask yourself which bottlenecks are most urgent to solve and in which policy areas or departments do people have the strongest interests to bring about changes?
- Make sure that gender impact assessment is no goal in itself but a starting point for change. Use the results to plan and implement concrete actions to improve your organisation and its practices.
- Always remember that transforming the mainstream is a step-by-step process. You will achieve the best results by an accumulation of carefully directed, far-reaching changes.[120]

2. Do combine gender expertise with knowledge of your organisation's businesses

Gender mechanisms cut through matters which are often taken for granted in your organisation. If you want to perform a gender impact assessment you need to have at least a basic level of gender expertise at hand.

- To increase the quality and reach of gender impact assessments, as well as their neutrality and objectivity, it may be advisable to assign them to external experts.
- Make sure that the results are accessible to all people in your organisation, including people with little or no experience in gender and diversity issues, by translating them into concrete recommendations.
- Promote the formulation of attainable and realistic recommendations by stimulating a fruitful interaction between gender experts and people well-acquainted with all aspects of your organisation.

3. Don't be afraid of far-reaching changes

Gender impact assessments may result in recommendations that require far-reaching transformations in the organisational structure of your organisation. Don't let yourself be discouraged by the resistance these changes may call up at first sight.

- Point out that the time and energy that may be involved in bringing about these changes are not wasted in the long term, doing nothing may cost your organisation much more, as argued before.
- Act as a role model in carrying out the recommendations and try to involve a critical mass of people by building ownership (see: § Ownership Building Tools).

CHAPTER 3

GENDER MAINSTREAMING AT UNIVERSITIES: THE PROCESS MODEL APPROACH

This chapter provides a process model to examine the quality and effectiveness of your organisation's procedures, products and services from a management perspective. Rather than focusing on the content of the university's core activities, it looks at the *management processes* necessary to perform these activities successfully. Based on the EFQM model[121] of excellence, nine dimensions of management are distinguished that are relevant for a smooth internal operation and external proliferation of your organisation. After linking these dimensions to the workaday context of universities, we will show you how gender mainstreaming can assist you in improving your organisation's performance in each of these areas. Gender mainstreaming enhances your ability to deal with the increasing heterogeneity in demands and ambitions in our global society: of students, employees, partners and stakeholders, male as well as female. It also provides handles to resolve the increasing tension between business and academic considerations that academic managers face today.

3.1 WHAT IS THE EFQM-MODEL?

The EFQM-model for excellence in business management has been developed by the European Foundation for Quality Management[122]. The model offers a framework to assess an organisation's progress towards excellent performance by differentiating between nine dimensions of management. Within each dimension, the model provides several criteria that indicate how to promote excellence. These criteria are neither normative nor prescriptive but rather descriptive: you can use them as handles to assess and improve existing management procedures in your institute and enhance the quality and scope of your organisation's products and services.

Five of the EFQM-management dimensions are called 'Enablers' and four of them 'Results'. *Enablers* cover the processes and conditions that allow your organisation to perform its key activities. They *are leadership, policy & strategy, people management, partners & resources and processes.* The *result dimensions* cover what the organisation actually achieves. They are divided into *customer results, people results, society results and key performance results.* The quality of the enablers is largely decisive for the results of an organisation.

The EFQM model for Business Excellence can be diagrammed as follows:

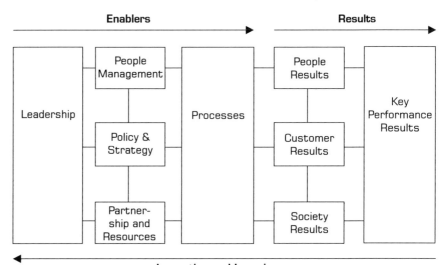

The arrow *'innovation and learning'* aims at the ongoing process of quality management. The EFQM-model is a circle or cycle-like model, embracing the idea of a continuously learning organisation. The business information you get from the result dimensions are used as feedback and input for the enabling factors of your organisation. Through this ongoing process of learning and innovation, your organisation will gradually move towards excellence. [123]

3.2   HOW CAN GENDER MAINSTREAMING PROMOTE EXCELLENT MANAGEMENT?

This chapter takes the EFQM-excellence model as a starting point towards mainstreaming gender equality in the management structures of academic institutes. Based on the EFQM-principles, a process model is developed for incorporating a gender perspective into all management dimensions and core activities of knowledge-organisations. Gender and diversity are seen as key issues in the evolution towards excellent management in universities.

In Chapter One we have described how processes like globalisation, internationalisation, hybridisation of research, expansion of education and the rise of market-oriented patterns of production urge universities to rationalise and innovate their management structures. We argued that the *transforming potential of gender mainstreaming* can help universities to deal with this challenge. In this chapter, we will further elaborate this argument by showing that there is a positive correlation between *quality-management* and gender mainstreaming. Both are based on the notion that organisations that internally reflect the diversity and complexity of their external environment can deliver more adjusted products and services.

The practice of integrating diversity into processes of quality control and quality management is becoming more and more accepted in managerial circles. In enterprises the idea gains weight that a diverse composition of the workforce positively affects the creativity within the organisation and helps to expand and improve sustainable networks with clients and society.[124] Several arguments were deployed in Chapter One that back this assumption for universities and related knowledge-organisations.

Although more and more managers may be convinced of the positive impact of diversity on the quality of their organisation, products and services, this has not yet been translated in a common *practice of implementing gender equality as a quality factor* in management models[125] - in universities even less than in business organisations. A tested case of the Affirmative Action Unit of the Belgian Federal Ministry of Employment and Labour has illustrated that this is a fruitful approach to improve the working climate, image and performance of your organisation as a whole.

Good Practice

Since 1997, the Affirmative Action Unit of the Belgian Federal Ministry of Employment and Labour – now called 'The Employment-Enterprises Unit'[126] – has been actively involved in integrating equal opportunities into business models that aim for total quality management. The Unit's efforts took place within the framework of the European project 'Putting the E into Quality – New Opportunities for Women'. In the context of this project, the unit linked the principles of the European Foundation for Quality Management (EFQM) to the issue of equal opportunities. The results of several test cases in a variety of more than 30 organisations – among which were SMEs, large private companies and non-profit organisations – were very encouraging. Thus, the Employment-Enterprises Unit in collaboration with several centres for quality management,[127] developed an expertise tradition in the practice of combining the equality issue with the quality management model of organisations. A brochure on 'How and Why' to integrate equality into the EFQM-excellence model was constructed to help managers apply this total e-quality paradigm.[128] A CD-ROM[129] on the rationale and the practical application of the model was put together, illustrated with various good practices from within all sorts of companies. An Equal Opportunities Network for private enterprises guarantees the disseminating- and learning-process. The Employment-Enterprises Unit also provides tailor-made consulting for organisations that want to grow towards business-excellence, including equal opportunities as a fully integrated quality-factor. To put the focus on best-practices in equality-integrated business-excellence an Equality-Award[130] was installed. This award is a special event organised every year to reward best gender-mainstreaming practising companies. Different European countries – Germany, Portugal, Italy, Spain and Ireland – are organising similar events. *The key philosophy is to build awareness and disseminate best practices by highlighting the excellent performance results of organisations integrating gender mainstreaming into their quality models.*

The process model for gender mainstreaming as presented in this chapter is inspired by the good practice of the Belgian Federal Ministry for Employment and Labour, though the model is altered and adjusted in order to attune it to the purpose of this manual: *gender mainstreaming in universities*. Gender and diversity are linked to the model in the form of guidelines to promote gender mainstreaming. They refer to the mainstreaming principles and tools as deployed in the previous chapters.

3.3   HOW TO USE THE EFQM-MODEL OF EXCELLENCE?

3.3.1   The nine EFQM-dimensions can be passed through in random order

The management dimensions as presented in the EFQM-model imply no specific order if it comes to finding a starting-point for mainstreaming gender equality into the organisations' management domains. You can choose any criterion as an entrance into the model. Your selection may depend on your function in the organisation, your personal interests or a specific bottleneck you want to address.

Example

A personnel manager is shocked by the statistics presented in the annual personnel reports showing that among the full professors only 5% are women. The manager, who is particularly worried since this low figure has remained unchanged for years, decides to set up a special programme concerning women and career planning. The manager, who is a part of the human resources department and an expert on personnel matters, chooses to enter the model via the criterion '*people management*', and to work on more equal opportunities in this management domain.

3.3.2   The EFQM-model can be used by anyone

Gender mainstreaming is not the privileged responsibility of managers or academic leaders. *Anyone in academia*, individual employees as well as policy makers, can find entrances into the EFQM-model to incorporate gender equality into the university's policies. You might be a scholar with an interest in gender mainstreaming, you might be a manager or policy-maker specialised in a specific domain (like HRM, finances, or communication), you might be an integral manager at a central or de-centralised level (Chancellor, Dean, Department Head, Head of a research team, etc.), you might reside as a staff-member in a decision-making board (such as appointment committees or educational programming commit-tees) or you might be a representative for a group of employees in the academia (a syndicate representative, a member of the works council, etc.). Whatever your position, you undoubtedly will be able to find an entrance into the model that is directly linked to the issues you are involved with.

If you want to handle a specific gender-related problem you can situate it in one of the nine management dimensions and use it as a starting-point for gender mainstreaming. It may be the case that you want to improve equal opportunities in your organisation but that you don't have enough information about the barriers your women colleagues encounter. In that case you can either: (i) start your activities from within a management domain where you suppose the culture and climate is open enough to introduce gender mainstreaming; (ii) you can do the opposite and start gender mainstreaming at an element of the model where you know that awareness building is necessary.

Example

At the opening meeting of a university's works council, the institute's Chancellor is invited to speak about the university's main policy topics for the coming academic year. A non-scientific member of the works council asks the Chancellor about his engagement concerning the issue of equal opportunities. The Chancellor replies that he would welcome and support initiatives concerning equal opportunities policies at the university even though it is not part of his current priority list of policy topics for the year to come. The member who asked the question knows now that the university board is open to suggestions. She provides the Chancellor with a list of gender-related problems at the university that has been compiled during the meetings of an informal university women-pressure-group. As the staff member knows that the management is open-minded to the gender-topic she uses the '*leadership*' entrance into the model.

3.3.3 The EFQM-dimensions are inter-related

As stated before, the EFQM-model is a *cyclic quality model*: the manage-ment dimensions as distinguished are inter-related and mutually supportive. Promoting excellence in one area is likely to affect the others positively. Processes of *feedback, innovation and learning* support the integral approach of gender mainstreaming: there will always be a gender-related topic that is relevant to another management area other than the one you used as an entrance into the EFQM-model.

Example

A survey on the future career plans of graduate students in a university's science department indicates, that the number of students planning on pursuing an academic career is worrying. The professor who initiated the survey is especially puzzled about the fact that the top five percent expressed little or no interest in an academic career. The main reason for this disinterest appears to be the poor invitational image of the science department as a workplace. The students criticise the science department mainly on two aspects: (i) the lack of women researchers, assistants and professors and (ii) the individual way of executing research. The professor, as the head of a research team consisting of five male researchers, decides to take action not only by trying to create better opportunities for women students in its own team, but also by informing the Dean and the University Board about the results of the survey.

The example above is a real bottom-up illustration of how equal opportunities may be integrated into the EFQM-model. The entrance is the *'customer results'* criterion. By communicating the alarming survey-results to the Dean and to the university top the professor makes the gender issue visible. Through a process of learning and awareness building a shift is initiated from equal opportunity issues in *'customer results'* towards other management dimensions, starting with leadership.

3.3.4   Different actors can start gender mainstreaming simultaneously

The list of nine management dimensions is not ordered, nor is it exhaustive. It can change, as organisations develop and innovate. Different university actors may well be working simultaneously on mainstreaming gender equality in different management areas. In that case, *co-ordination and communication* become crucial (see Chapter Two § Implementation &

Organisation).[131] If all actors are aware of each other's activities and communicate about them the chance grows that *co-ordination* becomes *co-operation*. To ensure that actions in different areas become mutually supportive it might be a good idea to work on installing a co-ordinating platform. This unit or network can be assigned with the task of structuring and monitoring all actions while sharing information and good practices. The designation of a responsible, co-ordinating person at central university level can be of great help, especially if this is an academic leader or manager with a significant voice in the university's decision-making process.

3.3.5 What if your organisation uses another quality management model?

If your organisation has already installed another model for quality management you will certainly be able to find elements that correspond to those of the EFQM-excellence model. When looking for an entry into implementing gender mainstreaming it is advisable to start focusing on *processes* – the organisation of research, education and scientific services – and *resources*. A lot of quality models mainly focus on the quality of products, services and production; they pay less attention to the organisational processes to obtain this quality.

In the university context, such quality criteria are based largely on international standards for measuring the quality of scientific research.[132] The quality of educational activities is generally evaluated by commissions consisting of (international) experts from a range of universities. They evaluate the content of programmes and existing teaching practices in universities and from this formulate recommendations for better organisation and management of the educational system, conforming to European standards.[133]

The additional value of the EFQM-quality model is that it explicitly links enabling management conditions to the results of an organisation, thereby emphasising the *dynamism* between different areas of management. The model addresses a broad range of areas in which excellence can be achieved. Many of these are becoming increasingly important for contemporary universities: academic leadership, knowledge management, building a learning organisation, sustainable networks with customers and other potential stakeholders and, finally, the perception of the organisation by its own employees and broader society.

The EFQM-model regards all these aspects as being as at least as important as statistical data about the number of products (e.g. publications, citations, graduations) and services (education, counselling, advice, etc.).[134] This is exactly why it lends itself so well to be used as a process model for gender mainstreaming. It provides useful handles to screen all management processes in your organisation by systematically wondering *by* whom, *for* whom and *about* whom they operate as they are and how they can be transformed to promote excellence and gender equality.[135]

Of course you cannot possibly review all nine dimensions of management at once. Gender mainstreaming is a long-term strategy that builds on a succession of mutually attuned actions in different disciplines and management areas. Its success depends largely on your ability to set priorities and mobilise people to act and react in a continuous process of change. The EFQM-model is open to innovation and organisational change. The exercise can also be done with respect to other issues in the area of diversity and social justice or in regard to currently emerging matters like environmental questions and ethical aspects of research and technology.

3.4 THE PROCESS MODEL: MAINSTREAMING GENDER EQUALITY IN ACADEMIC MANAGEMENT

1. ENABLERS

The following five EFQM-dimensions of management are *enablers*. Together, they provide the means and facilities necessary to keep your organisation going and enable people to perform their tasks successfully. Two of them, *people management and partners & resources,* provide the conditions needed for keeping up to the mark material and immaterial resources. The others – *leadership, policy & strategy and processes* – have a more steering or directive character: they assist the organisation in setting out and adjusting its strategic course, developing mechanisms to achieve its main purposes and mobilising people to support them.

The description of each management dimension starts with a brief summary of the criteria that according to the EFQM-model are essential to promote excellence. How these criteria relate to the academic context is illustrated most extensively in the paragraphs with respect to academic leadership and human resources management, two highly pressing issues in European university management. In the other dimensions we provide some handles for applying the model to the every-day context of your organisation by giving some examples of potential bottlenecks and ways in which gender mainstreaming can help you to solve them. Hopefully these examples inspire you to raise similar questions with respect to the other criteria thus moving you to systematically review the quality and fairness of all management processes within your institute.

1.1 Leadership

1.1.1 EFQM-criteria for excellent leadership

- Developing and articulating the organisation's mission, vision and values, and acting as a role model in creating a culture of excellence
- Shaping, executing and innovating management procedures
- Maintaining fruitful relationships with clients, partners and society representatives
- Motivating, supporting and valuing employers in their role, performance and ambitions.

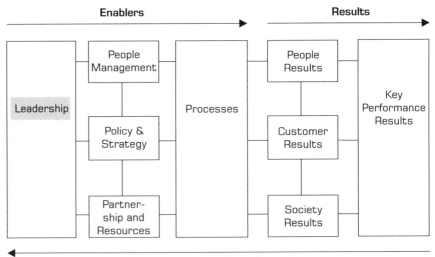

1.1.2 Leadership in the academic context

The quality of academic leadership is an important issue all over Europe. Universities are increasingly confronted with the need to rationalise management procedures due to developments like the rise of mass universities, the proliferation of research practices and the increasing globalisation and competition in academic research and education. All these changes have put the efficacy of traditional management structures – in which leadership was mainly in the hands of deans and professors, who guided the faculty's staff within the framework as set out by the university board – into question.

The current reorganisations of university structures in most European countries towards decentralisation, flexibility and hybridisation also demand new competences of academic leaders. In this respect, all four EFQM-criteria as mentioned in the framework above are important.

- *Developing mission, vision and values*: decentralisation implies that deans and professors are increasingly responsible for setting out the strategic course of their own institute or department. This requires strategic vision as well as having an eye for the ambitions and competences of all staff members. The university's mission and vision cannot be imposed by top-down regulation: they have to be supported all the way through the organisation.
- *Innovating management procedures:* the development of universities toward the 'power house' model involves a change in the style of academic leadership towards less directive and more coordinative management. Leaders must be able to respond adequately to internal and external developments and allow individual talents to flourish.
- *Relationships with clients, partners and society representatives:* external networks are becoming more and more important in view of the growing competition of commercial research institutes and foreign universities. Academic leaders cannot possibly promote their institute's interests properly without having built sufficient networks with national and international fellow institutes, funding agencies, publishers and channels to canvass potential students.
- *Motivating, supporting and valuing employers:* in most universities, the administrative aspects of personnel management are assigned to professionals in human resources management. But coaching as regards content and supporting the career building of academic staff members rests with senior scientists. Competences in this direction are crucial to combat the decreasing animo for careers in science and diminish the risk of being understaffed.

1.1.3 How to promote excellence in academic leadership?

The quality of academic leadership can be improved by making sure that all leadership competences as mentioned above are well performed in your institute. You can achieve this by three mutually attuned actions:

1. *Incorporating managerial competences as criteria in recruitment, selection and promotion procedures for senior functions in science.* Traditionally the criterion that is prioritised to measure the quality of candidates for senior posts in science is excellence in research. But to successfully manage a faculty or institute, other competences – like setting out strategic priorities, process management or improving the educational profile of the institute – are at least as important.

2. *Enabling residing academic leaders to regularly update and improve their management competences by establishing a coherent network of management development programmes and coaching facilities.* In most universities competence-building programmes are mainly concentrated on improving people's research qualifications. If you want senior scientists to act like modern managers you have to enable them to develop their leadership skills.

3. *Purposefully attracting and promoting scientists with additional competences to strengthen the power of your team.* If the residing professors in your faculty are primarily experts in the area of research – or indeed education – it is advisable to prioritise additional competences, such as network building or a drive towards innovation in the recruitment and selection of new scientific personnel.

In the current academic hierarchy, that ranges from Ph.D.-students to assistant professors, associate professors and full professors, many professors find themselves forced to perform managerial tasks at a cost to their development as top researchers and educators. To prevent this situation harming the competitiveness of your organisation a level of specialisation seems to be inevitable. A way to facilitate this is to create different career paths in science. Scientists could be allowed to specialise, at least to an extent, in research, education or management. To prevent the areas becoming too disconnected – which would affect their potential to mutually inspire and feed each other – conditions could be built in like the provision that all scientists have to spend a minimum percentage of time on activities besides their specialisation.

Another, partly complementary, option to release senior scientists from an overload of work is to facilitate task differentiation in academic leadership. Not all leadership tasks in science have to be per se performed by deans or professors: scientists in posts at the underlying levels may be very well capable of performing them with equal success. Actually, this is already a reality in many universities: many leadership and coordinating tasks that officially belong to the portfolio of deans and professors are, in fact, delegated to associate and assistant professors. In most cases, however, this distribution of tasks and responsibilities is not formalised. It has several advantages, though, to do put it down in black and white.

First, formalisation contributes to transparency in terms of responsibility and accountability. Moreover, since the distribution of responsibilities is clearly mapped out on paper you can easily check whether or not all leadership tasks needed for excellent management are covered sufficiently in your team. This provides a sound basis for a pro-active human resources management: it facilitates the search for additional competences and scientists can be effectively trained and assessed with respect to the specific tasks as described in their portfolios. In fact, these are the basic principles of *competence management,* an HRM-strategy that rapidly gains popularity in the business and non-profit sector and will be described in more detail in § 1.3 People Management.

The need to develop and mutually attune the management competences of senior scientists seems self-evident, but is not at all common in most academic settings. Some universities have started to offer management development programmes to academic leaders but this is not yet happening on a large scale, and usually these trajectories are offered on a voluntary base only.

Good Practice

The *Management Services unit* of the *University of Nijmegen* offers a voluntary, cost-free, training course to full professors in order to develop 'academic leadership' capacities. The course deals with management techniques and competences that are specifically attuned to the academic context. Based on individual development programmes, the participants are coached to implement these techniques and competences in their own work. Professors can follow the course individually as well as 'in-company' (together with other professors working in their unit or institute). The main themes of the course are:
– Developing strategic vision and implementing organisational innovation;
– Motivating and coaching staff members;
– Outcome-oriented leadership;

– Communicative techniques for successful negotiation, conflict resolution and performance assessments.

The Management Services unit offers similar courses to assistant professors and associate professors with leadership responsibilities.[136]

A potential explanation for the present lack of instruments to develop
(innovative) leadership skills is that in the academic culture – especially
at the top – coaching and training are surrounded by negative connota-
tions: as instruments to support 'weak' managers who need assistance to
perform well. Men seem to be more sensitive about these kinds of images
than women.[137] In Nijmegen, for example, the majority of professors par-
ticipating in the voluntary coaching programme (see above Good
Practice) are women, whereas men occupy a major share of the total
number of seats for professors. Rather than resting with the notion of the
professor who 'can do it all', it is far more constructive to reward the
readiness of these scientists to develop their managerial skills.

1.1.4 Gender mainstreaming academic leadership

The reflections presented above illustrate that improving the quality of
academic leadership also involves a re-thinking of the current pyramid
structure of science, that is featured by a one-sided focus on research competences. Gender mainstreaming assists you in this process by stressing
the importance of differentiated quality norms that allow a diversity of
male and female talents to flourish and are attuned to the specific
contexts in which scientists are operating: as researchers, educators or
managers (see § 1.3 People Management).

Apart from this qualitative dimension – that may be addressed by the
'gender proofing tools' as referred to below – there is also a quantitative
reason for mainstreaming gender equality in leadership. Universities that
do not fully use their female potential will be extra fiercely confronted
with the consequences of the impending retirement flow that will strike
hardest in the senior scientific ranks. Hence, gender mainstreaming in the
context of academic leadership involves two things: increasing the share
of women *in* leadership posts and promoting gender equality *through*
leadership.

1. Promoting gender equality in leadership

Until today, a gender balance in the highest levels has been hindered by the fact, that most top management positions in universities, such as Rector or Vice Chancellor, are occupied by scientists who gradually climbed to the top. Since women are underrepresented in senior grades in science their prospects of achieving such high positions are limited. Thus, increasing women's representation in higher scientific positions is a first step to promote gender diversity at the top. Function differentiation and a specified system of performance reviews and promotions are likely to overcome several of the barriers that female scientists face today since they increase the chance that scientists are appointed and promoted based on their competences rather than length of service.

- Promoting gender equality in academic leadership first of all involves *gender proofing all selection and promotion procedures* in order to remove barriers that currently hinder women's entrance into leadership positions (see §1.3 People Management).
- Also *the culture in academic management* needs to be gender proofed. The high turnover rates of female scientists indicate that the current academic culture does not equally fit the needs and demands of women and men. *Awareness and ownership building tools* (see Chapter Two § Awareness Building Tools) will help to promote a necessary change in mentality.
- As long as women and men are not equally represented *affirmative action measures* are useful to stimulate women's entrance into leadership positions. Two examples of such measures are actively headhunting female candidates and establishing temporary functions/appointments for women that allow them to qualify as 'professorable' scientists (other examples see § 1.3 People Management).

Illustration

The Aspasia Programme

In 1999 the minister of Education and Science in the Netherlands launched a national positive action programme to help women break through the glass ceiling in the sciences at the academic levels above the assistant professorship. This programme, named after the female Greek philosopher Aspasia, is executed by the *Dutch Organisation for Scientific Research (NWO)*[138] and all Dutch universities. Under the programme, female assistant professors (or junior lecturers) could apply for funding for either a four-year Ph.D.-project or a two-year post-doctoral project, linked to their own research issue. The *NWO* organises the normal peer review process and, in case of funding, the university promotes the assistant professor to associate professor (senior lecturer). The plan foresaw thirty Aspasia promotions in two tranches of fifteen, the first in 2000 and the second in 2002. In the mean-time the Aspasia Programme has proved to be an overwhelming success. Instead of fifteen, 68 women were promoted, bringing the percentage of female associate professors from 8.5% to 11%. An evaluation of the programme[139] revealed that its success was the result of a large quantity of high-quality applications on the one hand – alerting everyone involved in the underuse of women's potential – and the enthusiastic support by the NWO-Board on the other.

2. *Promoting gender equality through leadership*

Academic leaders have an important role in supporting and promoting the implementation of gender mainstreaming all the way through the organisation. Their high function enhances their ability to convince people that gender diversity hits the heart of the university and is a pre-requisite for promoting excellence in research and education. In words and deeds, academic leaders act as role models in creating a culture in which a diversity of interests and talents can flourish.

• Engagement of the top is expressed by *explicitly incorporating gender-mainstreaming targets in the university's mission statement*. Ideally, this commitment is echoed in all communications and policy measures of all university departments.

• Another indicator for the commitment of academic leaders is the extent to which gender mainstreaming is incorporated as a *prior task in the portfolios of top and senior officers*. To underline the seriousness of the matter, academic leaders should be regularly trained to enhance their awareness of gender issues and gender equality results should be incorporated in their performance reviews (see Chapter Two § Building Awareness & Ownership).

• University leaders are also responsible for establishing an *effective infra-structure* for gender mainstreaming. Mainstreaming demands sufficient means and facilities for planning, executing, monitoring and sharing information and expertise (see Chapter Two § Implementation and Organisation).

• By adopting *guidelines and codes of conduct* to which all members and employees have to sign up, academic leaders can promote that all people in the organisation are treated with respect and dignity. All forms of discrimination, harassment and bullying – whether on the basis of sex or any other ground – should be dealt with firmly. Accessible grievance procedures and sanctions are essential tools in this respect.

Illustration

Academic leaders act as role models in their own behaviour. Subtle forms of discrimination in the everyday customs of colleagues can be very troubling for 'lone' women at the top. After twenty-four years of service at the Stanford University's Medical Centre, the top neurosurgeon Dr. Frances Conley told the press in 1991:

"I resigned my position as a full, tenured professor because I was tired of being treated as less than an equal person. I was tired of being condescendingly called 'Hon' by my peers, of having my honest differences of opinion put down as a manifestation of pre-menstrual syndrome, of having my ideas treated less seriously than those of the men with whom I worked... I resigned because of a subtle sexism that, while not physically harmful, is extremely pervasive and debilitating".[140]

1.2 Policy & Strategy

1.2.1 EFQM-criteria for excellence in policy & strategy

- Exploring current and future needs and expectations of the organisation and its stakeholders.
- Identifying strategic aims and purposes and comparing them to current practices and performances.
- Elaborating, evaluating and adjusting policy and strategy.
- Demarcating key processes for implementation.
- Carrying out and executing policy and strategy.

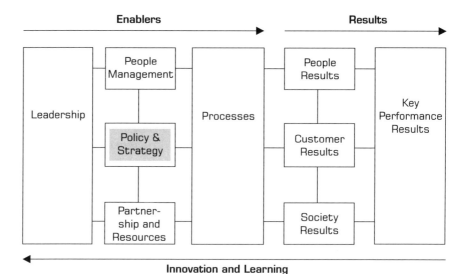

1.2.2 Policy and strategy in the academic context

Strategic plans and policy lines give concrete form to your organisation's mission, vision and values. If clearly articulated, your institute's mission statement provides a useful framework within which to set out strategic policy lines, targets, plans, objectives and processes. You can optimise the effectiveness of policy and strategy by regularly attuning them to internal and external developments that are likely to shape and alter your organisation's role and position in society. Smooth decision-making procedures, transparent implementation processes and commitment throughout the organisation increase your organisation's ability to respond adequately to the challenges of the time.

Universities can no longer afford to operate as isolated entities whose aims and actions are primarily steered by scientific-internal considerations. Challenges as described in Chapter One urge them to make strategic choices: they have to decide how they are going to react to developments like the rise of society-oriented research practices, the increasing international exchange of students and scientists and the European-wide implementation of the Bachelors-Masters structure. Since these choices will be partly based on internal strengths and weaknesses, an increasing heterogeneity is likely to occur in the European academic world.

This heterogeneity will give rise to new questions. Probably the most urgent matter concerns public accountability and democratic control. Who is responsible for deciding what kinds of research – and which areas of research – are invested in? Who is going to stimulate knowledge-building in areas where there are few or no wealthy foundations to fund research projects? These matters strongly affect the quality and content of academic research and, hence, hit the heart of the university. European institutes, national science foundations and universities have to agree soon how they are going to guarantee a healthy balance between fundamental research and applied, policy- and business-oriented research.[141]

In academic education, similar questions are likely to occur due to the expansion of commercial and demand-oriented educational practices. How will new forms of education, such as digital and contract education, affect the overall range of study fields in the academic world? Will educational institutes in areas less popular among students be able to survive the coming output-oriented demands of production? Which chances and possibilities – or risks – are involved in European-wide cooperation? Who is ultimately responsible for creating a balanced and high-quality offer of academic education?

Illustration

The Dutch National Research Foundation (NWO) has explicitly underlined the relevance of the questions mentioned above in its new strategy plan. One of the nine themes that NWO prioritises in the period 2002-2005 is "Ethical and Social aspects of research and education", thereby urging universities to incorporate ethical issues in their research and policy agendas. Hopefully gender-related issues will be treated as a spearhead in this thematic area: as argued below, the mainstreaming philosophy provides useful principles to address ethical and social questions in academic research and education.

1.2.3 Gender mainstreaming policy and strategy

Gender mainstreaming helps you to prevent a grinding down of academic practices by explicitly setting on the policy agenda ethical questions like: who decides and why? Whose interests are served by specific choices and practices in research, education and linking science and society? Gender mainstreaming urges you to break the myth of value-free science and calls for a democratic discussion on the themes and methods prioritised in research and education. The principles of fairness, justice, equity and democracy that underpin its philosophy help you to maintain quality and social responsibility in spite of the increasing competition and commercialisation within the academic world.

- When developing new strategies and policies make sure to *gender proof* them before final decisions are made. You can do so by performing a gender impact assessment (see Chapter Two § Gender Proofing & Evaluation) or by consulting gender experts (see ibidem).
- Gender mainstreaming implies that the *needs and interests of women and men are equally weighed and considered in all phases of the policy process*: preparation, decision-making, implementation and evaluation. In Chapter Two § Gender Proofing and Evaluation, a checklist is presented of relevant issues of attention in each stage of the policy process.
- Since all actors normally involved in policy making are responsible for implementing gender mainstreaming they need to be *trained in the working of gender mechanisms*. They also must consider it as their *task and responsibility to promote gender equality*. In Chapter Two § Building Awareness and Ownership, several tools are presented to build gender awareness and ownership.
- Apart from these measures – designed to incorporate gender equality in all regular policy programmes – *specific organisational conditions* are needed to initiate, stimulate and coordinate the gender mainstreaming process all the way through the organisation (see Chapter Two § Implementation & Organisation).

1.3 People Management

1.3.1 EFQM-criteria for excellent human resources management

- Realising and maintaining a balanced influx, mobility and turnover of personnel.
- Identifying, developing and maintaining the expertise and competences of individuals.
- Involving people by giving them responsibility.
- Initiating and facilitating a dialogue between the organisation and its people.
- Reviewing, acknowledging, rewarding and sanctioning people's engagement and performance.

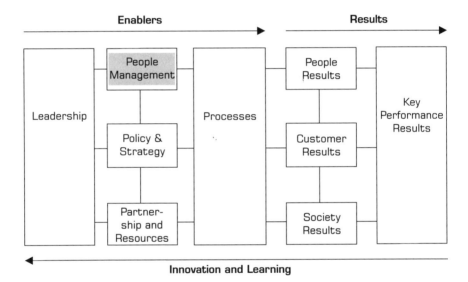

1.3.2 The need to increase mobility in the academic world

A pro-active human resources management system is indispensable for creating a balanced and satisfied body of personnel in which young and old, men and women, new and experienced, are all represented. This involves more than recruitment, selection and administration: people need to be stimulated and assisted to realise their plans and ambitions. Human resources management entails enlarging people's commitment to your organisation by giving them challenging responsibilities and allowing them to develop their competences conform their interests.

Until today, within most academic institutes, HRM has mainly consisted of personnel administration, like personnel planning and remuneration.

The often centrally regulated labour conditions offer little space for nego-tiation. Now that many national governments are drawing back from interference, universities get the chance to let go of the traditional, rigid models of personnel administration and make a shift towards more flexible, pro-active HRM systems.

The room to do so, however, is currently limited by the traditional academic hierarchy of functions, that prescribes a fixed proportion of junior and senior posts in science. Because of the relatively small number of senior posts in science many people lie in wait for promotion. The vacancies in senior posts that can be expected with the impending retire-ment flow will not structurally solve this problem. They will provide opportunities for some assistant and associate professors that are working in the right place at the right moment, but as long as the existing academic hierarchy is not transformed the next generation of scientists is likely to face the same barriers.

1.3.3 How to promote excellence in HRM?

The art of human resources management is to optimally utilise people's talents by matching the organisation's needs with the personal demands and ambitions of employees. This requires flexibility and mobility as well as investments to facilitate a process of life-long learning. Four kinds of actions are important to meet these conditions in the academic world.

1. Establishing facilities to increase mobility in science

A larger mobility in science will help to prevent de-motivation and unde-sirable turnover of talented scientists and will stimulate a healthy transfer of knowledge and technology. This is extremely important to remain competitive in the international research arena.[142] Several measures to increase mobility in science are:[143]

- *Function rotation*: permanent appointments under the condition that scientists internally change functions after a fixed period of duty, e.g. every five years;
- Linking the continuation of appointments in senior scientific posts to *regular performance reviews*;
- *Contract compliance*: contract appointments based on task descriptions, expected results and conditions for continuation in terms of quality and content;
- *Adding new posts* to the existing body of functions in science;
- *Increasing trans-frontier mobility of scientists* and (regional) cooperation

between academic institutes to facilitate collegial exchange, especially at EU level.

Good Practice

The TMR Marie Curie Fellowships

A good practice in promoting mobility in science was introduced by the European Community in its *Fourth Framework Research Programme (1994-1998)*.[144] The programme responds to the challenges of Europeanisation and globalisation by promoting three forms of mobility: exchange of researchers between universities, transnational mobility and horizontal flexibility or de-traditionalisation of academic career patterns.[145]

The *Community Research Training Grants Scheme (TMR-grants)* was designed to promote mobility of researchers throughout the EU and Associated States. The beneficiaries of these TMR-grants are called *Marie Curie Fellows*. The objectives of the TMR-grant system are described as follows: *'To promote the development and better utilisation of human resources in the Community through training and mobility of researchers'*.[146]

The Marie Curie grants scheme provides grants of four categories. Two categories focusing on *training*, more specifically providing training grants for doctoral and post-doctoral researchers. The grants are offered to researchers on both doctoral[147] and post-doctoral levels who want to receive training or specialise in a research institute abroad. Two other categories of grants are distributed. One focusing on grants for *established researchers* and one providing *return grants* for post-doctoral Marie Curie Fellows (see above: second category of training grants) from one of the designated 'less favoured regions'. The TMR Work Programme 1994-1998 contains guidelines on the distribution of these different categories of grants. At least 65% of the total funds goes to post-doctoral grants, a maximum of 20% goes to the doctoral researchers, a maximum of 10% goes to the return grants and a maximum of 5% goes to the established researchers. The doctoral and post-doctoral fellowships contain an age restriction of 35 years with allowances for applicants with career breaks for child-rearing, military service or because of physical disability.[148]

The TMR-programme focuses on all scientific disciplines providing grants for non-targeted, free research. Applicants must be nationals of an EU Member State or of an Associate State. Host institutions must be legal entities with their own research capacities. The duration of the different fellowships ranges from a minimum of three and a maximum of 36 months, depending on the kind of grant provided. Applications are evaluated by teams of independent scientific experts, appointed by the European Commission, and following a peer review logic. Evaluation criteria focus on the quality of the applicant, the scientific quality of the research project and the quality of the host institute.[149]

2. Offering attractive career prospects to scientists

Flexibility in itself is not sustainable. In 'The Futures Project' the European Commission warns of the risk of one-sidedly translating the aims of mobility and employability into the adoption of flexible contracts, especially temporary appointments.[150] The continuity of universities can be threatened if no investments are made in establishing attractive career prospects for scientists. Promising strategies in this respect are:

- *Letting go of fixed portfolios and the fixed proportion of junior and senior posts in science:* restitution of formal functions with flexible task descriptions increases the variety of career prospects in academic institutes and positively affects employability. Following the *'tenure-track system'*, as implemented in the US (see also Good Practice below), the promotion of individual scientists could be primarily based on their personal performances and competences rather than the availability of a function.
- *Facilitating specialisation in science:* scientists could be allowed a level of freedom to specialise in research, education or academic management (see also § 1.1 (academic) Leadership). This could help to increase the attractiveness of the university as an employer to a larger range of people: different career prospects appeal to multiple talents and ambitions.
- *Facilitating career steps to employers outside the academic world:* talented candidates could be refrained from pursuing a career in science by the idea – either false or just – that science is a dead-end path. Building networks and cooperation with business and non-profit organisations, e.g. by expanding counselling and advice practices, may help to break this image of the isolated university.
- *Offering flexible labour conditions that respect the principle of treating the employee as a whole person:* as illustrated earlier in this manual, today's employees no longer comply with the traditional breadwinner-homemaker model. Universities that want to create an attractive working environment will allow room for people's diverging demands

with respect to work-life balancing, roles in civic society and commitment to life-long learning (see also § 2.2 People Results)

3. *Setting up a coherent system of training, coaching, mentoring and competence building facilities*

An important aspect of HRM is the establishment of facilities to enable people to perform their tasks and ambitions properly. In most academic institutes, competence-building facilities are mainly focused on developing (research) methods and technologies, whereas other forms of coaching are at least as important, such as mentoring (introduction to networks and 'rules of the game'), supervision (reflection on own behaviour and competences) and collegial feedback (reviews on performance by near colleagues). Some professors may perform these tasks well but usually there is no coherent system of facilities to ensure that all staff members are trained and coached properly. In § 1.1.3. several competences were described that are relevant to build and develop in academic management. Examples of supportive tools in the other core businesses are:

- *Research:* training in research methods and technologies, feedback as regards content, coaching in publishing articles, training in communication and performance, introduction into important networks and structures, training in writing research proposals, building up research groups and managing them, facilitating international exchange of scientists;
- *Education:* training in educational methods and technologies, supervision of educational skills, training in group processes and diversity in the class-room, collegial exchange, feedback of students;
- *Linking science and society:* competence building in entrepreneurship, training in project management, budgeting, acquisition of finances, quality control, networking, popular writing, client satisfaction.

4. *Establishing fair and adequate recruitment, selection and promotion procedures*

In most universities, informal networks play an important role in the appointment of senior scientists. Sometimes even the unwritten rule prevails that candidates have to be invited to apply for a professorship. Practices like these limit the pool of potentials from which candidates are recruited. This is highly undesirable in view of the impending lack of academic personnel. Open recruitment procedures enhance the chance of finding the best candidates. The accuracy and fairness of selection and appointment procedures can be enhanced by:

- *Explicitly attuning selection criteria to the function and context:* rather than automatically prioritising excellence in research as the major selection criterion for vacant functions in science, it is more strategic to carefully map out which competences are most urgently required for which post. The increasing specialisation that is likely to occur in science stresses the need of looking for competences that are complementary to the residing staff's skills, not only as regards content – qualifications in either research or education – but also with respect to communicative and managerial competences.
- *Prioritising selection criteria in advance:* to prevent arbitrariness, selection criteria need to be ranked in an order of preference that is maintained all the way through the selection process. Agreeing on this order in advance – e.g. by consulting superiors and direct colleagues – helps you to counteract the personal preferences of appointment committee members as being more decisive than the interests of your institute.
- *Formalising assessment procedures:* strict selection procedures in which all steps needed to test a candidate's competences are put down in black and white are the best way to guarantee that candidates are selected on fair and equal grounds. To increase the objectivity of judgement it is advisable to involve one or more external members in appointment committees, oblige committees to report on their decisions and make these reports public.

It is not necessary to say that the facilities mentioned above need to be carefully attuned to the strategic course of the organisation. If your faculty board, for instance, has decided to increase external fund raising and society-oriented research, scientists need to be prepared for this task by competence building programmes in the area of networking, entrepreneurship, etc. *Competence management* is a proper model to facilitate such a pro-active attitude in HRM. The principles of competence management are rather simple.

It first of all involves a careful mapping out of all competences that are required for successfully performing the key tasks of your institute in research, education, science & society and management. This overview is used to compose competence profiles for individual staff members that are to be carefully attuned to each other to make them complementary. These competence profiles form the starting-point of HRM-policy: they are used as a base in recruitment, selection and promotion procedures as well as performance reviews. Performance reviews take place once a year and are not solely executed by superiors but also involve self-reflection and collegial feedback. The results are fed into the process of composing individual development programmess, which in their turn form the basis of the training and coaching that is offered to individuals.

Competence management is a cyclic model: individual competence profiles are regularly reviewed and adjusted to meet the organisation's strategic course, external developments and the competences of other staff members. This is how flexibility and responsiveness are built into the model. The reviews consist of questions like: are, by overall inspection, all tasks and competences needed for excellent performance covered sufficiently? Do individual staff members perform their tasks well? Is someone perhaps faced with an overload of work? Such a reflection may be helpful to address the bottlenecks as described in § 1.1 with respect to academic leadership.

It will also assist you in bringing to the fore other neglected areas in HRM. In many academic institutes, education is such an area. Often universities do not even demand basic certificates in education. Apparently this is perceived as something that anyone is capable of doing. This negligence does not only run the risk of under-utilising the talents of students, but could also damage the image of the university – both as an educational institute and as a future employer for students. It also has a gender impact, since generally female scientists are more involved in educational tasks than their male colleagues.

1.3.4 Gender mainstreaming human resources management

The current career system in science is especially disadvantageous to women.[151] Although women's entrance into science has grown significantly during the past three decades, their slow career progress and high turnover rates clearly signify that HRM policies urgently need to be 'gender proofed'. Progress to higher functions should depend on the quality of persons – assessed by clearly specified performance criteria and regular personal reviews – rather than the availability of senior positions.

Gender mainstreaming urges you to critically review quality criteria and define them in such a way that they allow room for diversity. This enables you to cope with the increasing task differentiation and specialisation that is likely to occur in science. Moreover, valuing and respecting diversity allows you to make optimal use of people's talents – including women's. This is indispensable in view of the combination of factors that, in the short term, will cause serious bottlenecks in the provision of academic personnel: the impending retirement-flow, the decreasing appeal for science and the growing international competition for good researchers.

Below, some strategies are presented to mainstream gender equality in HRM, grouped in three categories: (i) mobility (ii) competence development, coaching and career building (iii) recruitment and selection.

1. Mobility

Just as gender mainstreaming assists you in breaking one-dimensional notions of quality that hinder a necessary mobility in science, so the reverse is also true: transforming the pyramid career system – by function differentiation and increasing the mobility in senior ranks – is likely to facilitate women's progress in science. Some conditions have to be met, however, to ensure that women and men indeed are equal beneficiaries of these changes.

- New HRM policies and strategies provide a good opportunity to mainstream gender equality right from the start in their development. By applying a *gender impact assessment* in an early stadium you can prevent the creation of new barriers in the mobility of female and male scientists (see Chapter Two § Gender Proofing and Evaluation).
- *Systematically collected data on the internal and external mobility of male and female scientists* at all levels of the academic hierarchy provide useful information for the refinement and adjustment of HRM-policies. They show you which strategies are most effective and which levels or groups of scientists are faced with bottlenecks in mobility (see Chapter Two § Measurement and Monitoring).
- Statistics also provide a necessary ground for the adoption of *gender equality targets*. By integrating these targets in regular performance reviews and conditions for funding, you can stimulate efforts to promote women's mobility in science all the way through the organisation.
- *Affirmative action* measures are useful to give the mobility of female scientists an extra impulse. Some examples of these tools are:
  - creating temporary functions for women to increase their visibility as 'professorable' scientists (see illustration Aspasia-programme § 1.1 Leadership);
  - establishing research grants to promote women's progress in science;
  - setting up (international) databanks of talented and ambitious female scientists;
  - establishing prizes for excellent female scientists.

2. Competence development, coaching and career building

No matter which area you are working in, training and coaching are indispensable to keep your competences updated. We already have noticed that education and management are neglected areas of competence building and that the individual coaching of staff members is not a formalised practice in most universities. Gender mainstreaming urges you to transform good informal practices into formal procedures and facilities in order to promote equal opportunities for everyone. Employability and career prospects should not depend on the good will of individual professors, but on the talents of scientists – irrespective of sex or any other social dimension.

- Mainstreaming gender equality first of all involves pursuing the establishment of an *equivalent set of training, coaching and career building facilities in all core businesses.* The stronger emphasis that is currently laid on research does not only reflect a gender bias – since women are more often involved in education – but may also refrain people from specialising in education, management or science & society, even if they are actually more talented and interested in one of these areas.
- Gender mainstreaming also demands that women and men have *equal access* to all competence and career building facilities. Measurement and monitoring tools are useful to check whether or not this is the case. Women's participation could be stimulated by:
  – directly inviting women to participate;
  – regularly advertising in magazines and (digital) networks accessed by female scientists;
  – reserving a minimum number of places for female participants.

3. Recruitment, selection and promotion

Fair recruitment, selection and promotion procedures are essential to maintain a high quality body of personnel. They are also an important condition for gender equality: people are promoted on the basis of their competences rather than their gender or the personal preferences of appointment committee members.

- A logic first step to mainstream gender equality in recruitment, selection and promotion procedures is to *gender proof competence profiles* (see Chapter Two § Gender Proofing and Evaluation). Some relevant questions are: are the profiles formulated in gender-neutral terms? Do they address and attract a diversity of people? Are all the tasks and competences demanded actually relevant to perform the vacant function? Be especially alert to demands with respect to working experience: length of service is not directly related to a person's competences!
- Gender equality in *judgement* can be promoted by increasing the gender expertise of the members of selection and promotion committees and pursuing an equal share of male and female members. If there are not

enough female senior scientists in your institute you could attract a member from a fellow institute or aligning discipline.

- The *objectivity of promotion and selection procedures can be monitored* by systematically comparing the share of male and female applicants – at each level of the academic hierarchy – to the share of male and female candidates appointed. Another control mechanism consists of obliging the members of appointment committees to report the reasons for appointing or not appointing (female) candidates.
- As long as women are underrepresented their entrance into scientific positions can be promoted by *affirmative action* measures like:
  - actively headhunting female candidates, e.g. by contacting databanks or networks of female scientists;
  - explicitly inviting female scientists to apply;
  - preferential treatment of female candidates in cases of equal competences.

Good Practice

The *Research Centre Jülich* has established a special *Tenure Track Programme for the Promotion of Women Scientists*. For the women involved, the small-scale pilot is likely to enhance the attractiveness of their career prospects significantly:

'The basic idea follows the American tenure track concept, which outlines an academic career from postdoctoral researcher to a fixed-term professorship, culminating in a permanent contract. The centre uses this concept to give women a long-term perspective for achieving top positions in science at an early stage in their careers. Each year, beginning in 1999, three outstanding female scientists will be offered job opportunities as a group leader, initially with 2-year fixed-term contracts. This starting phase will be used to integrate the scientist into the institute's research programme and will enable her to develop her own working style. In the subsequent consolidation phase she will already be working on a permanent contract. During this phase she can expand and consolidate her research and personnel management experience so that she can qualify for leadership positions in science at the end of the 5-year programme. In addition, the centre aims to change the boundary conditions, and in particular make the research centre a more family-friendly working place.[152]

1.4 Partners & resources

1.4.1 EFQM-criteria for excellent management of partners & resources

- Building and maintaining external networks.
- Acquiring and managing financial resources.
- Managing buildings, equipment, material and non-material recourses.
- Developing and innovating methods and technology.
- Developing, innovating, and disseminating knowledge and information.

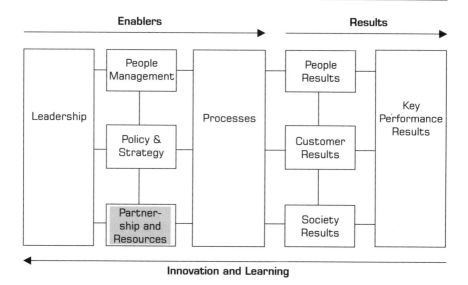

1.4.2 Partners & resources in the academic context

With the growing competitiveness in the academic world, pro-active strategies towards network building and external fund raising are likely to gain attention. Rather than waiting until external parties approach scientists for counselling or contract research, universities can also play an active, mediating role themselves. The need to promote excellence in managing partners and resources is stressed by developments like the rise of mass universities, globalisation, the growing demand for knowledgeable citizens and the increasing orientation on output-demands in research and education.

Hardly any university today can do without specialised communication and information services any more. Recruiting students and potential clients, building (international) contacts with publishers and fellow institutes and external fund raising are increasingly becoming businesses on their own. Even individual scientists cannot rely on their research competences alone: if they want to reach the top, contacts with journals, publishers, funding organisations and fellow researchers are indispensable.

Still, many scientists consider marketing strategies as being unworthy to the 'higher cause' of science. Universities that take the growing competition in the academic world seriously, however, will not allow this attitude to flourish. With the rise of the knowledge-society, academic institutes are gradually losing their monopoly position as sophisticated knowledge-building and knowledge-transferring institutes. Building sustainable networks with (potential) financers, partners and students is indispensable to survive the struggle with foreign universities and commercial research institutes.

The current decentralisation of university structures implies that individual scientists are increasingly responsible for managing their own partners and resources. They need to be provided with sufficient knowledge and information to perform this task successfully. A way to achieve this is to systematically incorporate skills as regards network building and resource management in competence building programmes, especially for academic leaders. Entrepreneurial practices could be stimulated by rewarding scientists who manage to tap new sources of revenue, e.g. by offering additional means to fund their projects up to a maximum percentage. Such strategies may help to bring about a change in mentality that is necessary to remain competitive.

Most universities have not yet formulated an adequate answer to the discussion that is currently going in the media about the potential risks and merits of commercial research funding. Avoiding this discussion will not help to solve the increasing tension between the responsibility of universities to protect the independence of academic research and their need to develop more business-oriented ways of production and organisation. Rather than allowing scientists to condemn entrepreneurial practices under all conditions, or leaving it to a process of trial and error, a more constructive answer lies in formulating concrete guidelines and conditions under which external funding is and is not allowed. Making these guidelines public and demanding all researchers, partners and clients to sign up to them will contribute to transparency, controllability and accountability.

1.4.3 Gender mainstreaming partners & resources

Scientists who condemn entrepreneurship in science by appealing to the principle of objective and independent knowledge-building forget for conveniently that academic agenda setting is a political practice anyway. As illustrated by the well-known motto 'knowledge is power', the themes and questions prioritised in academic knowledge are not neutral choices. Gender mainstreaming provides you with good arguments to break the traditional assumption that these priorities are scientific-internally given. Thus, it clears the way for an open discussion about knowledge, power and the distribution of resources in the academic arena. Discussing these matters is indispensable to be able to make a well-founded decision on the circumstances under which entrepreneurial practices are or are not desirable – with maintenance of quality – and how to guarantee a sufficient flow of resources to areas that are less easy to commercialise (see also § 1.2 Policy & Strategy).

It is important to see to it that women's voices are not marginalized in this discussion. As stated by the Etan Expert Working group on Women and Science: "Women constitute over half the population of the EU, they make a substantial contribution to the taxes that pay for the development of science and technology and are on the receiving end of outcomes derived from science policy."[153] Denying their experiences and perspectives runs the risk of losing an increasingly influential group of (potential) clients and stakeholders. Women need to be equal beneficiaries of the resources spent on the production and transferring of academic knowledge, as both participants as well as receivers.

1. Partners and resources in academic research

- Mainstreaming gender equality in research resources first of all involves a broad, *democratic discussion on the way in which financial resources are distributed over various research areas*. As illustrated earlier on in this manual, the skewed distribution of research resources over various disciplines reflects a gender-bias: generally, women are underrepresented in areas that receive the largest share of (public) funding and vice versa. A public discussion on priorities in research funding will positively affect the social justice and relevance of academic practices provided that various groups in community are equally represented in this discussion.
- Within academic disciplines, gender equality can be mainstreamed by pursuing an *equal distribution of financial means* – such as research grants and pay packages – over male and female scientists at all levels of the

academic hierarchy. In Chapter Two § Measurement and Monitoring, various indicators are provided to monitor whether or not these resources are equally accessible to women and men. If women appear to be disadvantaged, *gender impact assessments* can assist you in resolving biases that might be embedded in seemingly neutral procedures like peer reviews or pay negotiations (Chapter Two § Gender Proofing and Evaluation).

- Measures to promote gender equality in research resources should not only focus on the distribution of financial resources over women and men, but also on *other resources* like the room and quality of the working space, laboratory facilities, access to databases, membership of academies and editorial boards, informal networks and congress participation.
- An important way to increase people's access to research resources is to *exchange knowledge and information* on where and how to acquire them. Senior scientists have an important role in sharing their expertise in this respect that they can introduce scientists to relevant networks of potential partners, clients and stakeholders. Generally female scientists have less access to such networks than their male colleagues.[154] Institutionalising knowledge sharing and network building in this area will help to promote effective management of partners and resources all the way through your organisation.

Good Practice

The *Centre for Gender and Diversity* of the University of Maastricht has organised a *training course in writing research proposals and applying for research funds,* called the 'Onderzoeksatelier'[155]. The course, which is supported by the University Board, is primarily intended for female scientists at post-doc level or higher, although men are welcome as well. The candidate's research proposals range from individual post-doc applications to complete research programmes. The course consists of a series of workshops in which experienced and successful senior scientists offer personal coaching to the candidates in designing and proposing research projects. The major focus is not the content of the proposals as such, but content-related aspects relevant from a strategic point of view, such as:
- How to distinguish – and emphasise – the research relevance, scientific relevance and social relevance of research proposals?
- How to deal with expectations concerning dominant paradigms and quality norms?
- How to play in on the evaluation criteria of specific research grants?

In addition to this personal coaching, several joint training programmess are organised in which the candidates can acquire knowledge and skills in the area of fund raising techniques and strategies: know-how of national and international funding systems and foundations, writing successful proposals and building sustainable networks. If a research proposal is rejected a follow up project may be initiated in consultation with the candidate. The course has a double profit: it stimulates the application activities – and hence the career progress – of female researchers and is likely to enhance the acquisition of external research resources in the university as a whole.

4. Distribution of resources in academic education

- In academic education, the overall distribution of resources indicates a similar gender-bias as in research. A discussion on the *themes and areas of education that are publicly financed* is necessary to enable male as well as female students to flourish in a direction that suits them. A thorough reflection is also desirable to maintain a high-quality offer of academic education against the background of new, commercial forms of education, like digital and contract education.

- Within disciplines it is important to check whether or not male and female students *equally benefit from the knowledge and resources* offered to them. Special support services – like personal mentoring and coaching – could be established for groups that appear to systematically drop out at an early stage (see Illustration Mellow Project § 2.1 Customer Results). Such facilities will only be effective if they are combined with tools to bring about structural changes like gender proofing educational methods, curricula and study materials as well as training all educators in gender issues.

- Mainstreaming equality in educational resources also involves guaranteeing that women and men have equal access to *student services and facilities* like study grants, international exchange programmes, prizes, student-assistantships, network building facilities (congresses, councils, or committees), sports, housing facilities and information and advice services. In the process of designing these facilities and assigning means to them, the needs and interests of male and female students need to be equally weighed (see Chapter Two § Gender Proofing & Evaluation).

- All these strategies will help to establish an *attractive learning environment for a diversity of students*. This will give your organisation a head start in the competition for students that is pushed by the rise of output-based funding criteria.

Good Practice

Measures to ensure that women are equal beneficiaries of resources in academic research and education do not always have to take much time and energy. In the US a provision that is regularly used and appears to be rather effective is the refusal to finance congresses, seminars, and symposia if female and migrant speakers are insufficiently represented in the programme.[156] Similar provisions could be built into funding conditions for international exchange programmes, proposals for research and projects, study grants, etc.

1.5 Processes

1.5.1 EFQM-criteria for excellent process management

- Developing and managing processes to realise policy and strategy and monitor performance and quality.
- Improving and innovating processes to increase the satisfaction of clients and external networks.
- Developing and expanding products and services on the base of clients' needs and expectations.
- Managing the delivery of products, services, and external relations.

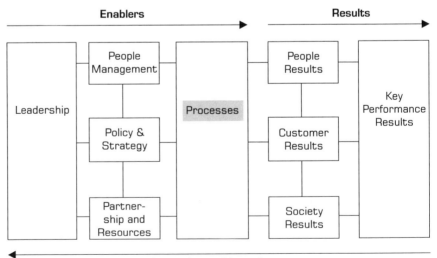

1.5.2 Process management in the academic context

Process management forms the spill of the EFQM-model of excellence: it links the enabling management dimensions to the results. Process management involves designing and improving organisational structures and procedures in order to guarantee an optimal achievement of the organisation's strategic goals, a high quality of products and services, and an optimal client satisfaction. Excellence can be achieved by continuously wondering: do the current processes in your organisation enable people to achieve the 'ideal' situation as identified in the mission statement? Do they need to be adjusted to improve the quality of products and services?

In the academic world, process management is complicated by several factors. One of them is that in most universities the core businesses are – for good reasons – not managed separately. Even if activities in research and education are institutionalised in separate units usually this distinction is not maintained in the portfolios of individual scientists. Without denying the surplus of a fruitful cross-fertilisation between research and education this hybridism complicates matters of responsibility and accountability.

Who, for example, is ultimately responsible – and accountable – for adjusting educational programmes and methods in order to increase their attractiveness to a diversity of students: male and female, black and white, old and young, heterosexual and homosexual? Even if this goal is explicitly prioritised in your institute's mission statement it might fall into the background of a more general tension between the research and education tasks of individual scientists and their specific interests and expertise. Who controls whether your institute's strategic aims and targets are achieved and who gets the bill if they appear to be not?

Another challenge academic institutes are faced with is the need to develop processes that can deal with the ongoing clash between the traditional academic paradigm of science as a realm of independent knowledge-building and the business paradigm that urges universities to adjust the organisation and production of science to demands regarding output and social relevance. Experience has learned that a separation of tasks between scientists and specialised managers – e.g. in HRM or communication – can only partially solve this problem. Administrative managers often operate according to another rationale than scientists which may lead to tensions or, in the worst case, conflicts of authority.

Illustration

An exploring study for the national *Advisory Council for Science and Technology* in the Netherlands showed that equal opportunity policies in Dutch universities have partly failed due to this tension.[157]

In the 1980s and '90s, Dutch universities were confronted with a succession of radical reforms in reaction to the rapid growth of education that resulted in enlarged bureaucratic sectors. This development intensified the traditional conflict between scientists and bureaucrats, or professionals and managers, and caused meshes in the net of equal opportunities policies. This was especially the case in recruitment and selection procedures for scientific posts: professors claimed the authority of judgement – in itself not unjustly – on grounds of scientific quality and content. In this, however, they often disregarded measures, guidelines and quota that were set up by HRM-managers in line with the university's strategic policies to establish equal representation of men and women in science. Professors appealed to traditional concepts such as academic liberty and impartial science. In the process, equal opportunities policies and positive action measures became marginalized – or enclosed – in the personnel departments in universities where policy makers were only allowed to deal with social measures such as day care and women's personal career plans and not with the core activities of the university: research, teaching, and how to change gender relations there.

The introduction of integral management – an important pillar of the decentralisation processes in many European universities – is likely to prevent a bureaucratic tug of war between scientists and organisational managers but at the same time it calls for measures to spare academic leaders from an overload of work. Moreover, since decentralisation enhances the flexibility of individual departments to grow and develop as they wish – conforming to the idea of the 'power house' – a diffusion of organisational structures is likely to occur within academic institutes. This diminishes the power of the central university board to appeal to the responsibility of individual departments to carry out common policy lines or pursue a basic corporate identity.

All these factors illustrate that good process management is getting more and more important to promote excellent performance in the academic context. The power-house model can not survive on a collection of strongly specialised scientists alone: you also need translators and integrators who are able to work in multi-disciplinary teams and who are well equipped to combine diverse research results, knowledge demands and applications.[158] This entails establishing new organisational structures, stimulating the (inter-disciplinary) mobility of scientists and facilitating partnerships with business and public organisations.[159] Above all, it requires new management procedures and good process managers.

1.5.3 Gender mainstreaming process management

The art of process management is to find the right balance between regulation and flexibility. Fixed procedures contribute to transparency but could also be a burden to the flexibility and creativity of your organisation. Gender mainstreaming assists you in designing processes in such a way that they respect potential differences between people and take into account the different contexts in which they are operating. If applied well, gender mainstreaming promotes a situation in which all the organisation's activities are designed and informed by knowledge of the diverse needs and expectations of their (potential) beneficiaries.

- Gender mainstreaming first of all involves promoting *transparency in procedures and outcomes.* All procedures – e.g. with respect to appointments, promotions, research funding, coaching, competence building, labour conditions or pay packages – need to be put down in black and white and made public. They need to be accompanied by gender-segregated statistics and effective grievance procedures to ban all forms of direct or indirect discrimination.
- Mechanisms for *participation, consultation and democracy* assist you in establishing flexible processes that are responsive to internal and external needs and expectations. Gender mainstreaming demands that women and men are equally involved in these mechanisms. Specialised units, centres or gender experts can be consulted for advice, information and good practices of gender mainstreaming (see Chapter Two § Building Awareness and Ownership).
- Processes in your institute can be freed from one-sided norms and criteria by systematically submitting them to *gender impact assessments.* The Dutch 'EER' (see Chapter Two § Gender Proofing and Evaluation) is a tested tool that, step-by-step, guides you through the process of designing gender proof policies and processes.
- Just as gender mainstreaming will help you to improve the quality of process management, so good process management will contribute to the effectiveness of gender mainstreaming. As argued in Chapter Two § Implementation & Organisation, tools and strategies for gender

mainstreaming need to be carefully attuned to each other as well as to the current structures and practices in your institute. This requires an eye for context as well as strategic vision. In other words: it requires good process management.

Illustration

The following examples illustrate that the answer to the question: 'What is the best way to mainstream equal opportunities?' varies from organisation to organisation and from country to country. Top-down approaches to stimulate equal opportunities in science appeared to be very effective in Sweden but were less successful in Denmark and the Netherlands.

In Denmark, it would have been advisable to combine the government's equal opportunities programme with awareness building tools to promote a change in mentality within universities.

The Danish government's programme to advance women's participation in senior positions in science showed large resemblances to that of the Swedish government: both programmes consisted of a large number of mutually attuned measures which were partly obligatory. While the programme booked significant results in Sweden, it was far less successful in Denmark. One of the reasons was that in Swedish universities government intervention is much more accepted – and in many cases even expected – while in Denmark the programme provoked strong resistance from an influential group of senior scientists.[160]

In the Netherlands, the ineffectiveness of the government's initiative was caused by a lack of sanctions and a negligence of current transformation processes in university management structures.

In 1997, the Dutch government adopted the 'WEV'[161], a law that obliges universities to set targets and develop plans for promoting women's representation in senior posts in science. Until today, the results of this law have been minimal. This is partly caused by a lack of sanctions – either positive or negative – but has also to do with the fact that the top-down, regulative character of the 'WEV' contrasts with the decentralising forces within universities that were initiated by a law adopted the same year: the so-called 'MUB'[162]. Due to the reorganisations in the context of the 'MUB', the central boards and bureaus of Dutch universities lost a great deal of their regulative power – including their regulative power with respect to gender diversity and equal opportunities: most responsibilities were transferred to faculties, institutes and service units who were supposed to operate as autonomous units. This trend towards decentralisation was at odds with the top-down rationale of the 'WEV'[163]

2. RESULTS

The following EFQM elements are *result dimensions*. How your organisation is doing in *customers, people, society and business results* reflects in a way your performance in the enablers as presented above. The results of your organisation can serve as feedback to promote excellence in the enabling dimensions through processes of learning and innovation. In the following paragraphs, several aspects of customers, people, society and business performance are outlined within the academic context. A range of tools is provided for perception measurements and indicators for the university's performance in these different areas.

The result-dimensions are not only useful in processes of promoting a learning organisation and innovating management procedures. Their importance is also underlined by the increasing demand for accountability and public control. As the financing structures of universities grow more and more towards performance-based funding, managerial ways to measure results and make the performances of universities visible and comparable will gain attention.

2.1 Customer Results

2.1.1 EFQM-criteria for excellent customer results

- Measuring clients' perception of the organisation by means of polls, surveys, user's groups, delivery scores and procedures for compliments and complaints;
- Using the results as input to improve the organisation's image, the quality of products and services, logistics, advise, technological support and loyalty.

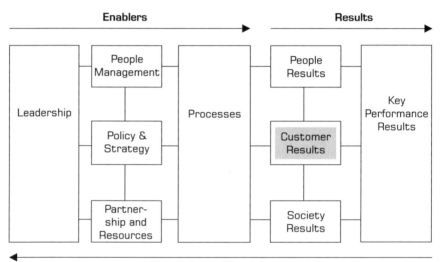

2.1.2 Customer results in the academic context

In the context of the growing competition, universities seek to distinct themselves from others. The increasing globalisation and the rise of the multicultural society urge them to pay attention to diversity in their marketing strategies. Universities could use diversity management as a quality promoting strategy in addressing their customers. Good customer performances are a trump card for any organisation, linking aspects of motivation, performance and quality of services.

The range of potential clients in the university's mission of *attracting and executing research* has expanded significantly during recent decades, especially with the rise of applied and society-oriented research practices. All actors in the public realm are potential customers, ranging from governmental institutes, intermediate organisations – like trade unions and

employer's organisations – and non-profit organisations, to private institutions. Serving a broad variety of audiences is a key factor for success in
linking science and society. Since strategies to improve your organisation's
results in this area are extensively dealt with in § 2.3 Society Results, this
paragraph will mainly focus on *customer results in education:* students' satisfaction and performances.

In the educational practice of universities, the ongoing shift towards
customer-oriented thinking is illustrated by the fact that internal and
external evaluations on the quality of educational systems in general
and of teaching practices in particular, never take place without inter-
viewing students. Evaluations like these are becoming more and more
important in recruiting new students: high scores enable universities to
promote their image as attractive educational institutes in the outer
world.

The relevance of measuring student's satisfaction and monitoring the
quality of education is likely to increase in view of the European-wise
endorsement of the Bachelor-Master system. Common standards and
accreditation systems are essential to allow for comparison with foreign
institutes. In the near future accreditation is likely to play an essential
role in the provision of certificates, titles, study grants, quality labels etc.
This, combined with the modern practice of output-oriented funding,
stresses the urge of developing sophisticated indicators to measure
student's satisfaction and performances in education.

You can optimise your institute's pedagogic performance by installing
processes in which customer results serve as feedback for innovation and
learning. Such processes could consist of:

- Making sure that the results of *standardised student evaluations* concerning the quality and content of educational courses are used as *feedback
  in individual performance reviews* with educational staff members.
- Using the results of these evaluations as *input for composing individual
  development programmes* for the educational staff; all teachers need to be
  sufficiently trained in progressive pedagogic methods, personal
  coaching and communicative skills.
- Establishing *codes of conduct* as regards teaching practices and interaction between teachers and students to which all students and scientists
  have to sign up.
- Setting up university-wide *procedures for compliments and complaints* concerning the content of curricula, student services, teaching methods
  and competences, practices of discrimination, harassment, or bullying,
  examinations, evaluation procedures etc.

- Performing university-wide *surveys* among students and old-students to assess how they experience(d) the educational system as regards accessibility, communication, flexibility, innovative quality, mentoring and coaching practices etc.

Good Practice

University of York, UK

The University of York in the UK has a particularly customer-friendly website, welcoming its students with a broad range of information as regards *student associations, information services* (such as libraries and computing services), *study information, support services* (student counselling, disability adviser, chaplainry, welfare information officer etc.) and *miscellaneous*, among which are details of complaint procedures and equal opportunities policies for students.

Concerning the *Equal Opportunities Policy for Students*, the following *Statement of Policy* is made:

'The University of York is committed to the active pursuit of an equal opportunities policy which addresses the need and right of everyone in the University to be treated with respect and dignity in an environment in which a diversity of backgrounds and experiences is valued. It aims to ensure that no prospective or existing student should receive less favourable treatment on any grounds, that are not relevant to academic ability and attainment. The University has a continuing programme of action to bring about the implementation of its policy.'

A *Code of Practice* with respect to equal opportunities and the university can be consulted on-line, providing information on:
- The aims of the equal opportunities policy
- Student admissions policy
- Monitoring programmes
- Teaching, learning and assessment procedures
- Widening participation (meeting the needs of particular groups of students, e.g, people with disabilities, students with domestic and caring responsibilities)
- Facilities and services (all should operate in accordance to the university's equal opportunities policy)
- Supervisory system (clear procedures and advice, in accordance to the equal opportunity's policy included in handbooks)
- Special religious and cultural needs
- Harassment (Code of Practice on Harassment)

- Complaints procedures (if someone feels being treated in a way that is not consistent with the equal opportunities policy one should contact the Equal Opportunities Advisor, the Vice-Chancellor or the Senior Admissions Tutor)
- Responsibility for equal opportunities (Equal Opportunities Committee, with students' representatives and with advisory responsibilities in the Council of the University; Equal Opportunities Advisor)
- Contact persons

http://www.york.ac.uk/np/students.htm

2.1.3 Gender mainstreaming customer results

New, client-oriented, types of education and market-oriented production patterns stress the importance of satisfying the educational needs and expectations of a diverse population of students. It does not take an expert's eye to recognise the possible impact of a one-sided male dominance in the educational staff. Gender mainstreaming customer results in education involves:

- Making sure that the results of all student evaluations, surveys and procedures for compliments and complains are *systematically segregated by sex*. Comparing the answers of male and female students allows you to uncover potential gender biases in educational products and services which need to be addressed to enhance the overall customer's satisfaction.
- Explicitly including questions with respect to equal opportunities and diversity into all student evaluations, polls and surveys. The results indicate whether your organisation's *gender mainstreaming activities are visible and effective* and in which areas an extra impulse or transformation might be necessary.
- The customer-friendliness of educational products and services can be enhanced by *training all educational staff members* in dealing with (gender) diversity and having an eye for students' diverse needs for coaching and mentoring.
- Apart from these integrative strategies, a *forum or ombuds(wo)man* could be assigned with the specific task of assessing the (gender)-friendliness of the learning environment and dealing firmly with all forms of unwanted behaviour.

Good Practice

One of the main aims of the Centre for Equal Opportunities Policies of the University of Leuven is the installation of a *debate forum on equal opportunities* within the university with specific procedures to deal with comments, suggestions and complaints. In 1999 the *'Meldpunt Gelijke Kansen*[164] was installed. At this forum every member of the university, students as well as personnel, can lodge complaints, make suggestions and mention everything they think is relevant to the topic of equal opportunities policies at the university. The forum exists both virtually and materially: it can be addressed via the website of the Centre or by personally contacting (by e-mail, telephone or face-to-face) the Consultant and the Chancellor's Advisor.[165]

Good Practice

A good example of the client-oriented approach in the field of education is the *Mellow Project*. 'Mellow' is an acronym for *Life LOng MEntoring of Women* in or towards technical jobs. It is designed to increase the involvement of women and girls in advanced technological education. The Mellow project has been executed within the framework of the LEONARDO DA VINCI programme, which is the European Commission Action's programme for the implementation of a European Community Vocational Training Policy.

Mellow entails four actions:

1. Students (girls) from secondary schools go out into the technical field for a day with a female engineer in order to get a realistic view of her work.

2. Female students in higher technological education are coached by an experienced female engineer during their transition from education to employment. The period of mentoring covers a time span of six months before graduation until at least six months after graduation.

3. Junior female engineers are coached by experienced female engineers in the development of their careers.

4. The mentors involved in the two previous actions are trained by special programmes that have been developed during the project.

Mellow started in 1995 as a Pilot Project within a partnership of institutions of five European countries. After successfully accomplishing this Pilot Project, a Multiplier Project has been started with partners in

eight European countries. The aims of this Multiplier Project are:
- enlarging the existing network to other countries;
- exploring new challenges for the existing partners;
- setting up a European Information Collection Centre on the Internet;
- further developing the theoretical assumptions and matching the possibilities by database systems on the Internet;
- organising a conference on mentoring.

In 1998, the *Mellow Good Practice Handbook*[166] was published providing a description of how to develop and successfully implement mentoring projects. The handbook provides practical recommendations, good practices with respect to mentorship as well as evaluation checklists.

http://www.vhto.nl/mellow/

2.2 People Results

2.2.1 EFQM-criteria for excellent people results

- Monitoring people's perception of the organisation by means of polls, works councils, interviews and regular performance reviews;
- Installing processes for learning and innovation: using people results to enhance people's satisfaction, competences, productivity, motivation and involvement.

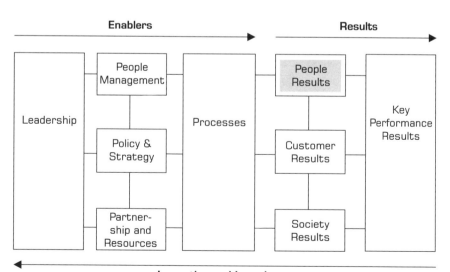

2.2.2 People results in the academic context

Measuring results concerning the academic workforce covers gaining information about people's *motivation* and *satisfaction*. All aspects of academic careers and the organisational structures and cultures that relate directly to people's chances and position in your organisation need to be taken into account to achieve excellent people results. People results provide an important *indicator for the quality of your organisation's HRM strategies*. Since European universities suffer from a considerable gap between need and supply of human resources, increasing the attractiveness of scientific careers and keeping people satisfied are essential managerial tasks in academic institutes.

Another important aspect of people results relates to *working conditions*. Among modern employees there is an increasing demand for flexible work-life balancing arrangements. This demand is at odds with the prevailing work attitude in most universities that is still implicitly based on the notion of the full time working breadwinner. Part-time work is not at all common, certainly at the top. Neither are facilities like dual appointments, flexible working hours or parental leave. Universities that offer their academic personnel more freedom to choose their own balance between work and private life will find that this is a winning card in increasing people's satisfaction and enhancing their own attractiveness as employers: the labour market increasingly consists of employees – women as well as men – who prefer a part-time appointment of three to four days a week to a full-time contract.[167]

Also the institute's *culture, customs and ethics* are essential in monitoring people's perception of the organisation. These do not only include the values, mission and vision that are officially carried out by the top but also informal manners and codes of behaviour. As argued in Chapter Two (§ Gender Proofing organisational culture) ideally the climate in an organisation functions as a binding factor that actively engages people with the organisation's goals and identity. But if the culture does not allow for diversity, it may very well have an exclusionary impact as well, which is highly undesirable in view of the growing competition for good researchers.

Regularly surveying your workforce on how they feel about the elements mentioned above provides you with useful information on how to promote an attractive working environment and excellent labour conditions. You can do so by means of surveys, works councils, regular performance reviews or exit interviews. Another important source of information is data about people's performance and participation in the organisation. Several relevant indicators are:

- *Human resources management:* do people feel motivated by their opportunities in selection and promotion procedures, career planning, prospects for specialisation, knowledge building, competence development, coaching and feedback, network building, peer relationships etc.?
- *Working conditions:* are people satisfied about personnel facilities like administration, work-life balancing arrangements, health and security conditions, childcare facilities, pay and benefits, job security, sabbatical leave, exit conditions etc.?
- *Organisational culture:* do people feel comfortable with current practices in the area of leadership, daily customs and practices, respect and dignity, communication, transparency, empowerment, recognition, involvement, democracy, equal opportunities, innovative power and the organisation's role in society?
- *Performance and participation:* how do people perform in terms of productivity, grants, certificates, graduations, participation in decision-making, peer reviews, suggestion schemes, advise and consultation, membership of commissions, response to people surveys, organisation of and participation in congresses and seminars, number of grievances and complaints, turnover rates, absenteeism, sick leave, etc?

Whatever mechanisms you use to measure people's satisfaction and perception of the organisation, it is essential to establish *processes for a smooth dissemination of the results* to relevant actors all the way through the organisation. If a senior scientist, for instance, receives a complaint about a shortage of child-care facilities or computing services during a performance assessment, it is important to report this immediately to the HRM- or ICT-service involved, thus feeding a process of learning and innovation.

Good Practice

University of Cambridge, UK

During the summer of 2000, *Cambridge University* commissioned a major audit of its policies and practices in the area of people management, conducted by specialist consultants *Schneider-Ross*.[168] According to the Vice-Chancellor: 'The audit sought to develop a clear view of the position and perceptions of different staff groups in the university – men, women, members of white and ethnic groups, and people with disabilities – to check on the operation of existing policies and procedures and to work towards furthering a culture in which all members of staff are enabled to maximise their own development and their contribution to the university's success.'[169]

The input to the audit report included:
- A study of policy documents and staffing statistics;
- Face-to-face interviews with individuals (stakeholders and individuals from all staff groups);
- Focus groups of men, women, ethnic minority staff and staff with disabilities;
- A questionnaire sent to all staff which secured an above average 40% participation rate and which was consistent across all staff groups.

The results of the audit were explicitly used to *initiate processes of innovation* all the way through the organisation. The audit formed the basis for specific recommendations and an action plan that currently is in the process of implementation. The main areas wherein the recommendations and action plans for change are situated, are:
1. Communication and further building the case for change
2. Putting the strategy in place for the 'new agenda'
3. Building leadership and management capacities
4. Taking a radical look at career progression processes
5. Breaking the assumptions about working hours and processes

In the context of *improving people's satisfaction,* the recommendations concerning career progression and working processes are particularly outstanding. The planned or already existing actions regarding these topics are:
1. Building in specific guidance around career progression – conducting appraisals etc. prioritising staff development, appraisal, mentoring, accountability, valuing staff and work-life issues.
2. Carrying out a detailed review of the criteria used in the senior lecturer appointments, identify concerns, sharing these with those involved and putting in processes to avoid such issues in the future. Later on extending this to all academic promotions processes.
3. Ensuring requirement for equality monitoring data is effectively built into all recruitment, promotion and leaving processes.
4. Re-looking at the criteria for progression ensuring administrative and management skills figure appropriately
5. Reviewing the existence of any age-related criteria for appointments.
6. Setting up a process to ensure that all staff in under-represented groups are mentored from the outset of their careers.

7. Carrying out a systematic review of the potential for extending part-time working in academic roles. It will be important to continue facilitating and monitoring the take-up of the various schemes already in place. While success here is likely to be a measure of cultural change, enabling all categories of staff to achieve better, healthier and more productive work-life balance will also be a part of the culture change itself.

http://www.admin.cam.ac.uk/offices/personnel/equality/

2.2.3 Gender mainstreaming people results

Gender mainstreaming explicitly pursues a culture of democracy, dignity and respect for diversity that are all essential to commit employees to your organisation and make them feel comfortable. The principle of treating individuals as whole persons urges you to review your institute's working conditions on flexibility that will enhance your organisation's ability to meet the needs and demands of a diversity of people.

By segregating the results of all surveys, works council reports, and performance reviews by gender you can monitor whether male and female employees are *equally satisfied* about the HRM-facilities, working conditions and organisational culture in your organisation.

• Apart from gender-specific data about people's satisfaction, it is also important to monitor whether women and men *are making equal use* of the provided services in the area of HRM, working conditions and participation.

• If either women or men appear to be under-represented as users or satisfied employees, *gender-proofing tools* will help you to resolve gender biases that refrain people from optimally developing their talents and competences or pursuing the work-life balance they prefer. This will positively affect the overall people results in your organisation.

Illustrations

Fairness in funding
Swedish Medical Research Council (MRC)

In 1997, the Swedish researchers C. Wennerås and A. Wold published an article in the scientific magazine *Nature*, exploring why male applicants at the Swedish Medical Research Council (MRC) were twice as likely to be granted a post-doctoral positions than female applicants.[170] The article, based on an empirical study of the peer review system, indicated that three factors were independently decisive for the height of a candidate's score on 'scientific competence': the applicant's scientific productivity, affiliation with a member of the peer review committee and the applicant's sex. Male applicants appeared to receive higher competence scores than female applicants with the same scientific productivity: female scientists had to be 2.6 times more productive than their male colleagues to be perceived as equally competent. The article in *Nature* had an important awareness-raising effect: procedures that were assumed to be objective were proved to be not by hard evidence. The publication lead to extensive discussions in scientific and popular media and inspired similar studies in other countries.[171] In the Swedish MCR, measures were taken to resolve the signalled (gender) bias: more female evaluators were introduced as well as strict guidelines and procedures to reduce injustice in the assessment procedure. Increasing the fairness of procedures contributes to the quality of judgement, since the chance is enhanced that the best applicant is selected.[172] Eventually, this will positively affect the organisation's overall people results.

***

Marie Curie Fellowships

Another study concerning equal opportunities in the field of scientific research funding was carried out with respect to the female participation in the Marie Curie Fellowship programme (see also Good Practice § People Management), called *'The Participation of Women Researchers in the Training and Mobility of Researchers (TMR) Marie Curie Fellowships'*[173] The researchers in this project examined the barriers to the training and mobility of female researchers and the extent to which female researchers have the disposal of sufficient knowledge of the European grant schemes mentioned above.[174] A great deal of the study is dedicated to the impact of the mobility requirements on female participation in the Marie Curie Fellowships. Career progression in science and (international) mobility have been interconnected for some time now. The study provides thorough information and research data supporting the assumption that the mobility requirements, characteristic for the TMR-grants, have a gendered impact. They only appeal to a specific part of the scientific population, ruling out many women, especially those partnered and/or parenting.[175]

2.3 Society Results

2.3.1 EFQM-criteria for excellent society results

- Monitoring how society perceives the organisation by means of polls, reports, public meetings, representatives of the community, government institutes;
- Reviewing the organisation's role model with respect to social responsibility, participation in society, facilities to prevent health and security risks and environmental pollution, contributions to maintain natural resources;
- Developing processes that facilitate an adequate response to social developments, public opinion, good will of government institutes, and that help to improve the organisation's reputation in society.

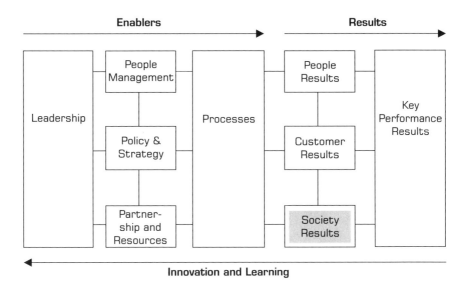

2.3.2 Society results in the academic context

With the rise of the knowledge economy, measuring society's perception of academic knowledge-building and transferring practices is becoming more and more important. Every university has a core activity in *linking science and society*. In this process, the local community and the national and international society should be informed about specific scientific research results, through intermediate organisations and other informing mechanisms. 'Science' can be perceived as a public good, funded by society in order to benefit the public.

Current processes of professionalisation – e.g. medicalisation, scientification, mediatisation – increase the impact of science on society. Specialists from different disciplines, mostly academics from respected institutes and universities, are consulted for sharing their knowledge and their views on ongoing public debates. Thus, scientific institutes have the power to partly shape and reshape the public's perspective on social, sometimes very delicate, issues like racism, euthanasia, impact of medical and technological developments or scenarios in international relations. Through processes of communication and consultation, scientists can give an important impulse to raising social awareness and setting priorities on the public and political agenda.

Information on society's perception of the organisation can be obtained from surveys, reports, public meetings, governmental authorities etc. The following items derived from the EFQM-excellence model are relevant as it comes to academic institutions and their public image:

- *Social responsibility:* how does the institute perform as regards disclosing information to the community, acting as a role model in promoting diversity and equal opportunities, impact on local and national economies (e.g. employment, R&D), relationships with government authorities and ethical behaviour?
- *Involvement in society:* to what extent is the organisation involved in offering education and training, medical and welfare provisions, technological advice, scientific expertise, and voluntary or non-profit services to a broad range of members in society?
- *Activities to prevent nuisance and harm from the organisation's activities:* are sufficient precautions taken to prevent health risks, accidents, noise, toxic pollution, and security risks (e.g. in scientific laboratories); are infrastructural arrangements (housing, campus facilities etc.) provided to cope with the increasing number of student and scientist inhabitants; are activities developed for the preservation and sustainability of resources as regards mobility, ecological environment etc.?
- *Image and performance in society:* to what extent is the organisation's reputation expressed in the form of quality labels, rewards, prizes, number of references and quotations in public media, and frequency of requests for research, counselling and advice?

Collecting data as described above will only make sense if it is used as *input to promote excellence in the enabling facilities* that are related to it. If the scientists in your organisation, for instance, appear to be less frequently quoted in public media than their colleagues in fellow institutes you can improve your organisation's society results by training scientists in network-building, public writing and communication strategies. Such processes of feedback and innovation are increasingly important to commit a diversity of society actors – public, private and non-profit organisations – to your organisation as potential partners and clients in contract research and education.

2.3.3 Gender mainstreaming society results

Gender mainstreaming will positively affect your organisation's society results since it explicitly aims to break dominant concepts of scientific quality – e.g. that fundamental research is more important than applied or society-oriented research or that dissemination of knowledge within the scientific forum is more important than exchange in information to a broad public[176] – that hinder a fruitful interaction between science and society. Given their public responsibility as knowledge-building and transferring institutes, universities act as role models in promoting gender equality and diversity.

- Whether academic institutes perform this role model successfully is first of all expressed by the *composition of the scientific staff and student population*: to what extent are different groups in society – categorised by gender, race, sexual orientation, religion, ethnicity or age – equally represented?

- Another indicator for the level of gender equality in society results is to monitor whether women and men are *equal beneficiaries* of the university's activities as regards *social responsibility and involvement in society*. To be able to measure this, all society results need to be systematically segregated by gender and compared to each other.

- In areas of under-representation, *awareness and ownership building tools as well as gender proofing measures* are essential to promote excellent society results. Universities can improve their image in the outer world by making their efforts to promote equality and diversity known to the public and regularly reporting on the progress they make.

2.4 Key Performance Results

2.4.1 EFQM-criteria for excellent key performance results

> – Monitoring the organisation's performance in all core business in terms of quality of products and services;
> – Measuring financials and market results;
> – Using these results as feedback for innovating policy & strategy, processes, partners & resources, HRM, leadership and knowledge management.

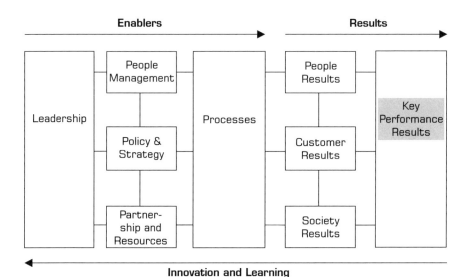

2.4.2 Key performance results in the academic context

The last EFQM-dimension to monitor an organisation's performance concerns the overall *'business-results'*. They reflect the institute's performance in all core activities and are, to a large extent, decisive for the continuity of the organisation. In academic institutes, the main indicators for these results are the input, processes, and output in academic research, teaching, and linking science and society.

Public control mechanisms urge universities more and more to rationalise management procedures and operate like modern business organisations. This also involves an increasing attention to comparable, numeric standards to monitor the university's key performances. Several standards as derived from the EFQM-model are:

• *Financial results:* turnover, budget compliance, results, net profit;

- *Marketing results:* market share (student share, orders in research, counselling, and advice), progression towards commercialisation (contract education, contract research), volume of production (number of graduates, publications, citations);
- *Processes:* management performances, productivity, time and means spent to planning, execution, evaluation and innovation;
- *Partners and resources:* number of external clients and partners and their added value, number of products and services brought in by partners, number of joint projects and innovations;
- *Buildings, equipment, and material:* usage, supply, consumption, replacement;
- *Technology:* innovation grades, intellectual ownership, patents, royalties;
- *Knowledge and information:* accessibility, integrity, social relevance, utility and exchange, value and intellectual capital.

In most universities the administration and management of these key performance results are largely assigned to professional managers and service units. But with the introduction of integral management the expansion of commercial teaching practices – like contract and digital education – and the rise of contract research, it becomes more and more important for heads of academic departments to have at least a basic notion of marketing strategies and financial management. Scientists involved in society-oriented and applied research are increasingly required to manage their own projects and finances. In the near future, facilities to specialise and build competences in this direction are inevitable to remain competitive in the academic arena.

Procedures for measuring the quality of key performances, however, cannot be restricted to numeric output standards alone. Apart from the traditional *science-internal criteria* – like the internal and external consistency of theories – a major challenge for the near future is to develop qualitative standards that take into account the *social, cultural and political impact* of academic practices. The growing interdependency of science and the public realm stresses the need for assessing the *social relevance* of academic practices. The peer review system does not necessarily answer this demand. Standards need to be developed on how society can inform science policy and vice versa (see also § 2.3 Society Results).

2.4.3 Gender mainstreaming key performance results

Key performance indicators in the context of universities need to recognise the added value of diversity and equal opportunities in teaching, research and linking science and society. In the previous paragraphs we have already explained how gender equality and diversity can be incorporated in customer and society results. The art of measuring key performances is to bring these aspects together into multi-dimensional quality criteria, combining comparable, numeric standards with qualitative criteria as regards content and social relevance. This corresponds to the gender mainstreaming ideal that all science policies and practices are informed by the diverse needs and expectations of their potential beneficiaries. You can achieve this by systematically passing trough all stages of the process model as deployed in this chapter: acting and reacting, step-by-step, following a random order of preference, strategically building a long-term process of transformation.

SUMMARY

1. In the first chapter of the manual the history of the concept *gender mainstreaming* is briefly outlined. This definition of the *Council of Europe form 1998* is taken as starting point for further deployment of the concept, including issues at stake, responsible actors and main prerequisites and principles of the gender mainstreaming strategy.

'Gender mainstreaming is the (re)organisation, improvement, development and evaluation of policy processes so that a gender equality perspective is incorporated in all policies and at all stages by the actors normally involved in policy-making'

Policy initiatives since the EU declaration of 1996 concerning the merits of gender mainstreaming are briefly commented.

2. The relevance of gender mainstreaming in the context of universities is shown by linking recent changes and challenges in the European academic world with key success factors of the gender mainstreaming strategy. The transforming and innovative potential of gender mainstreaming is connected with changes like the rise of the powerhouse model within universities, the growing market demands for flexible, high qualified and knowledgeable people, the call for accountability and public control concerning research funding and research results and the growing need for pro-active managerial strategies in academic organisations.

3. Chapter Two looks at the core-businesses of universities summarised in three main activities: providing education, executing scientific research and providing scientific services to society. Gender mainstreaming can be introduced at universities through four categories of tools and instruments applied to these three core activities. The four sets of tools are: (i) *measurement & monitoring*, (ii) *implementation & organisation*, (iii) *building awareness & ownership and* (iv) *gender proofing & evaluation*.

4. The practical use, merits and profits of the tools are illustrated by several examples, illustrations and good practice cases from the academic world. An overall illustration of how you can transform your organisation towards more gender diversity and with a quality heightening effect is

provided by the Deloitte & Touche Business Case.

5. Chapter Three takes a challenging perspective on universities as organisations that – in response to the recent changes as outlined in Chapter One – are in the middle of innovation processes concerning their managerial ways and practices. A 'Business Excellence Model' as developed by the European Foundation for Quality Management (EFQM) is taken as a framework for introducing gender mainstreaming in universities' management. The EFQM-model distinguishes nine different management elements and sets out criteria for achieving excellence in each of these nine elements. By integrating gender equality as a quality heightening criterion into each of the nine managerial categories, the model offers an alternative way for looking at academic organisations, their core activities and their management, their quality procedures and the opportunities gender mainstreaming can offer in this respect.

6. The status of this manual is not at all final. Since the main purpose of the project *'Equal Opportunities at Universities. Towards a Gender Mainstreaming Approach'* is to exchange experience and expertise on the subject of gender mainstreaming and universities, the manual resulting from these activities (01/07/2000-30/06/2001) is to be considered an interim report. Feedback, reviews and commentaries will be appreciated, since this will undoubtedly improve the use and implementation of the manual.

7. The *follow-up* of the project will be concentrated on the contextualisation of the manual among the EU-Member States and their academic institutions. Good practice examples from other Member States, elements from the legal frameworks concerning equal opportunities policies, from the different academic practices and gender mainstreaming expertise will optimise the manual. The same goes for the language. As several reviewers argued, a translation of the *'Manual on gender Mainstreaming at Universities. Equal Opportunities at Universities. Towards a Gender Mainstreaming Apporach'* into several Member States' languages will be necessary within the contextualisation process.

NOTES

Chapter I: What is gender mainstreaming and why is it a key to success?

1. Council of Europe, *Gender Mainstreaming. Conceptual Framework, Methodology and Presentation of Good Practices*. Strassbourg, Council of Europe, May 1998.
2. Council of Europe, (1998), *op.cit.*, p. 12.
3. The full texts of the Beijing Declaration and Platform for Action are available at: http://www.un.org/womenwatch/daw/beijing/
4. In each area of critical concern, the *Beijing Platform for Action* specifies various strategic objectives. In the area of education and training, several strategic objectives are formulated concerning science and technology. These objectives vary from the development of curricula and teaching material to multidisciplinary courses for science and mathematics teachers to sensitise them to the relevance of science and technology to women's lives.
5. COM (96) 69 final.
6. It announced its intention to do so in its progress report on the follow-up of the communication: COM (98)122 final.
7. COM (1999) 76.
8. European Council Resolution, adopted 20 May 1999 (OJ C 201/1 – 16.7.1999). European Parliament Resolution, adopted 3 February 2000 (PE 284.656).
9. Max Planck, Institute for Biophysical Chemistry, Göttingen.
10. European Commission (Osborn, M., Rees T., Bosch, M. et al.), *Science Policies in the European Union. Promoting Excellence through Mainstreaming Gender Equality. A Report from the ETAN Expert Group on Women and Science*. Luxembourg, European Commission, Office for Official Publications of the European Communities, 2000.
11. This report is currently in production. **See**: Commission of the European Communities, *Women and Science: the Gender Dimension as a Leverage for Reforming Science*. Brussels, Commission Staff Working Paper, 15-05-2001, SEC (2001) 771.
12. On 8-9 July 1999 the Commission organised a conference called Networking the Networks, which resulted in a declaration (Women and Science: Networking the Networks. *Declaration of Networks Active in Europe,*

Brussels, July 8&9, 1999) and in a network guide (available at: http://www.cordis.lu/ rtd2002/science-society/women.htm).

13. Recent numbers show that overall this target has not been achieved yet but that it certainly gave a significant impulse to women's representation in many panels. **See**: Commission of the European Communities, (2001), *op.cit.*, annex 5.

14. This presentation will take place at the conference Gender and Science, organised by the European Commission, in Brussels on 8&9 November 2001.

15. This summary is based on: European Commission (Osborn, M., Rees T., Bosch, M. et al.), (2000), *op.cit.* **and on**: Rees, T., Gender Mainstreaming. In: Watson, S., & L. Doyal, (eds.), *Engendering Social Policy*, Milton Keynes, Open University Press, 1998:1, p. 165-183.

16. Rees, T., (1998:1), *op.cit.* **See also** recommendations from: Centrum voor Gelijke Kansenbeleid K.U.Leuven, *Gelijke Kansenbeleid en Universiteit. Naar een Mainstreaming-benadering. Eerste Gelijke-Kansenrapport K.U.Leuven*, Leuven, Centrum voor Gelijke Kansenbeleid, Oktober 1999.

17. Rees, T., *Mainstreaming Equality in the European Union*. London, Routledge, 1998:2. **And** Rees, T., *Women and the EC Training Programmes: Tinkering, Tailoring, Transforming*. Bristol, University of Bristol, SAUS Publications, 1995.

18. Lamoen, I. van, *Gender mainstreaming: een goed begin is het halve werk. Een inventarisatie en evaluatie van het emancipatiebeleid aan Nederlandse universiteiten. In opdracht van de Katholieke Universiteit Leuven*. Nijmegen, 1999.

19. Commission of the European Communities, *Making a Reality of the European Research Area: Guidelines for EU Research Activities (2002-2006)*. COM(2000) 612, Brussels 4-10-2000.

20. Adviesraad voor het Wetenschaps- en Technologiebeleid (AWT), *Halfslachtige Wetenschap. Onderbenutting van vrouwelijk potentieel als existentieel probleem voor academia*, AWT-Advies Nr. 43, Den Haag, AWT, 2000.

21. Bosch, M. (red.), I. Hoving & G. Wekker, *In het hart van de wetenschap. Naar total E-quality en diversiteit in de universiteit.*AWT-Achtergrondstudie Nr. 15, Den Haag, Sdu Uitgevers, 1999. **And**: Adviesraad voor het Wetenschaps- en Technologiebeleid (AWT), (2000), *op.cit.*

22. Keijzer, B.S.C. & E.H. Gordijn, *Resultaten arbeidsmarktenquête jonge wetenschappers*. Ondernemingsraad Projectmedewerkers NWO en landelijk AIO en OIO Overleg, 2000.

23. Vucht Tijssen, B.E. van, *Talent voor de Toekomst. Toekomst voor Talent. Plan van aanpak voor het wetenschapspersoneelsbeleid*. Utrecht, 2000.

24. For example a post-doc salary in the US is comparable to that of a professor in the Netherlands. **See**: Vucht Tijssen, B.E. van, (2000), *op. cit.*

25. Vucht Tijssen, B.E. van, (2000) *op.cit.*

26. European Commission (Osborn, M., Rees T., Bosch, M. et al.), (2000), *op.cit.*, p.7-20. **See also**: Portegijs, W., & M. Brugman, *Eerdaags Evenredig? Belemmeringen en beleid ten aanzien van de doorstroom van vrouwen naar hogere wetenschappelijke functies.*Beleidsgerichte Studies Hoger Onderwijs en

Wetenschaps- beleid, Den Haag, 1998.

27. Bagilhole, B., & J. Goode, The Contradiction of the Myth of Merit, and the Reality of a Patriarchal Support System in Academic Careers. A Feminist investigation. *The European Journal of Women's Studies*, 8, (2001), 2, p. 161-180.

28. Georgi, H., Is there an unconscious discrimination against women in science? *APS News*, (2000), p.8. **and** Zimmermann, K., *Spiele mit Macht in der Wissenschaft. Passfähigkeit und Geschlecht als Kriterien für Berufungen*, Berlin, Edition Sigma, 2000.

29. Valian, V. *Why so Slow? The Advancement of Women. Carrier Patterns of Women Academics are Slow due to Lack of Support and Inadequate Information.* Cambridge, Massachusetts, MIT Press, 1999.

30. European Commission (Osborn, M., Rees T., Bosch, M. et al.), (2000), *op.cit.*, p.23.

31. Portegijs, W., & M. Brugman, (1998), *op. cit.*

32. Portegijs, W., *Jammer dat u gaat: het snelle verloop van vrouwelijke wetenschappers: een lek in het emancipatiebeleid.* Utrecht, 1993.

33. Fruytier, B. & V. Timmerhuis, *Mensen in Onderzoek. Het mobiliseren van HRM in wetenschapsorganisaties.* Assen, Van Gorcum, 1995.

34. Brainstormsessions at Maastricht University, 19/3/2001 & 4/4/2001, with Drs. Anneke Eurelings, Prof. Dr. Hans Philipsen, Prof. Dr. Cor Spreeuwenberg, Prof. Dr. Paul Tummers and Dr. Liesbet Van Wely.

35. Centrum voor Gelijke Kansenbeleid K.U.Leuven, *Vooronderzoek. Gelijke Kansen bij aanstelling, benoeming en bevordering van het Zelfstandig Academisch Personeel aan de K.U.Leuven*, Leuven, Centrum voor Gelijke Kansenbeleid, Juni 2000, p.50-52.

Chapter II: Gender mainstreaming at universities: The instrumental approach

36. Meyerson, D.E. & J.K. Fletcher, A Modest Manifesto for Shattering the Glass Ceiling, *Harvard Business Review*, (January-February 2000).

37. Based upon and excerpts taken from: (i) McCracken, D. M., Winning the talent war for women: sometimes it takes a revolution. *Harvard Business Review*, 78, (November-December 2000), 6, p.159-167. (ii) Flynn, G., Deloitte & Touche changes women's minds. *Personnel Journal*, 75, (April 1996), 4, p.56-68.

38. CEO stands for Chief Executive Officer.

39. McCracken, D.M., (2000), *op.cit.*, p.167.

40. McCracken, D.M., (2000), *op.cit.*, p.164-166.

41. Equal Opportunities Commission (EOC), *A good practice guide. How to set targets for gender equality.* Manchester, Cardiff and Glasgow, EOC, January 2001.

42. McCracken, D. M., (2000) *op.cit.*, p.162.

43. Area Development Management (ADM), *A manual for gender mainstreaming the local development social inclusion programme 2000-2006*. Dublin, November 2000, p.14-15.

44. Based upon recommendations from: European Commission (Osborn, M., Rees T., Bosch, M. et al.), (2000), *op.cit.* **And**: Federaal Ministerie van Tewerkstelling en Arbeid (MTA), Directie Gelijke Kansen, *Mainstreaming in het federaal tewerkstellingsbeleid. Evaluatie en statistische hinderpalen*. Brussel, MTA, december 2000.

45. European Commission (Osborn, M., Rees T., Bosch, M. et al.), (2000), *op. cit.*

46. Equal Pay Task Force, *Just Pay. A report to the Equal Opportunities Commission*. Manchester, Equal Opportunities Commission (EOC), 2001. For more information, see: www.eoc.org.uk

47. Equal Pay Task Force, (2001), *op. cit*, p. ix.

48. Equal Pay Task Force, (2001), *op. cit*, p. ix.

49. This figure was copied from: European Commission (Osborn, M., Rees T., Bosch, M. et al.), (2000), *op. cit.*, p.13 & p.137-138.

50. Rees, T., (1998:1), *op.cit.*

51. Braithwaite, M., *Manual for integrating gender equality into local and regional development*. Brussels, Engender, 1998, p.29-35.

52. Rees, T., (1998:1), *op.cit.*

53. Rees, T., (1998:1), *op.cit.*

54. Nelen, S., Mainstreaming als 'nieuwe' strategie inzake gelijke-kansenbeleid: wondermiddel of verdwijntruc? *Tijdschrift voor Genderstudies*, 3, (2000), nbr. 4, p.33-42.

55. McCracken, D. M., (2000), *op.cit.*, p.160.

56. McCracken, D.M., (2000), *op.cit.*, p.166.

57. European Commission (Osborn, M., Rees T., Bosch, M. et al.), (2000), *op.cit.*, p.67.

58. Area Development Management (ADM), (2000), *op.cit.*, p.21-23.

59. Braithwaite, M., (1998), *op.cit.*, p.29.

60. *Centrum voor Gelijke Kansenbeleid K.U.Leuven, Gelijkekansenbeleid en Universiteit. Naar een mainstreaming-benadering. Eerste Gelijke Kansenrapport K.U.Leuven*, Centrum voor Gelijke Kansenbeleid, Juni 2000, p.12-13.

61. Universiteit Utrecht, Bestuurscommissie Emancipatiebeleid, *Vooruit v/m*, utrecht, 1998, p.35-44.

62. Based on recommendations from: (i) Fitzgerald, R., *Toolkit for Mainstreaming Equal Opportunities in the European Structural Funds. A practical Guide to plan Preparation and Implementation*. Glasgow, Equal Opportunities Commission (EOC) & HERA 2001, 2000. **And**: (ii) European Commission (Osborn, M., Rees T., Bosch, M. et al.), (2000), *op.cit.*, p.65-70.

63. Quoted from: Bosch, M. (red.), I. Hoving & G. Wekker, (1999), *op.cit.*, p.177-178.

64. SWOT-analyses stands for an analyses of strenghts, weaknesses, opportunities and threats (e.g. regarding women's opportunities in personnel

management, diversity in the class room, etc.)

65. Nelen, S., (2000), *op.cit.*, p.35-36.

66. Based upon recommendations from: (i) European Commission (Osborn, M., Rees T., Bosch, M. et al.), (2000), *op.cit.* and (ii) Equal Opportunities Commission (EOC), (2001), *op.cit.*

67. Benschop, Y., & M. Verloo, *Gender in Balans. Mainstreaming gender in perso-neelsmanagement, In opdracht van en in samenwerking met de dienst Emancipatie-zaken van het Ministerie van de Vlaamse Gemeenschap.* Brussel, 1999, p. 36-41.

68. See: http://www.kuleuven.ac.be/gkg/

69. Rees, T., (1998:1), *op. cit.*

70. Fischer, A., *Normen, waarden en gedrag in de organisatie. In opdracht van het Ministerie van Landbouw, Natuurbeheer en Visserij.* Den Haag, 1999.

71. Fischer, A., *De top (m/v): de paradox van emoties.* Amsterdam, 1998.

72. See: Buikema, R., M. Meijer & A. Smelik, Postmoderne cultuur en repre-sentatie. In: Brouns, M., M. Verloo & M. Grünell (red.), *Vrouwenstudies in de jaren negentig. Een kennismaking vanuit verschillende disciplines.* Bussum, 1995, p.79-108. **And**: Verbiest, A., *Zaken zijn zaken. Taal en de kwaliteit van beleid.* Den Haag, Ministerie van Sociale Zaken en Werkgelegenheid, 1999.

73. **See**: Crum, M., & J. Bal, *Werk- en loopbaanpositie van postdocs.*Leiden, Research voor Beleid, 1998. **See also** illustration about the Dutch Ministry of Social Affairs in Chapter Two § Gender proofing and evaluation.

74. McCracken, D. M., (2000), *op.cit.*, p.162.

75. McCracken, D. M., (2000), *op.cit.*, p.163.

76. McCracken, D. M., (2000), *op.cit.*, p.163-164.

77. See: http://www.cews.uni-bonn.de/

78. More information at http://www.athena.ic.ac.uk

79. McCracken, D. M., (2000), *op.cit.*, p.162.

80. Leistungsorientierte Mittelvergabe an Hochschulen unter Berücksichtigung des Landesgleichstellungsgesetzes. See § 5 Gesetz zur Gleichstellung von Frauen und Männern für das Land Nordrhein-Westfalen (Landes-gleichstellungsgesetz – LGG) vom 09-11-1999.

81. See: § 5 Hochschulrahmengesetz.

82. See: Gesetz über die Hochschulen des Landes Nordrhein-Westfalen (Hochschulgesetz – HG) vom 14-03-2000, § 5 HG-NRW.

83. See § 5 Landesgleichstellungsgesetz NRW.

84. McCracken, D. M., (2000), *op.cit.*, p.167.

85. McCracken, D. M., (2000), *op.cit.*, p.167.

86. Portegijs, W., & M. Brugman, (1998), *op. cit.* **And**: Noordenbos, G., Genderassymetrie in de aanvraag van onderzoekssubsidies. *Tijdschrift voor Genderstudies*, 2/4, (1999), p.36-45.

87. **See**: Wennerås, C. & A. Wold, Nepotism and Sexism in Peer Review. Com-mentary. *Nature*, (1997), 22. **And**: Brouns, M., *De kwaliteit van het oordeel. Een onderzoek naar sekse en beoordelingssystemen van NWO en KNAW.* Utrecht, Nederlands Genootschap Vrouwenstudies, 1999.

88. Equal Pay Task Force, *Just Pay,* Manchester, Equal Opportunities

Commission (EOC), 2001.

89. Massachusetts Institute of Technology (MIT), A Study on the Status of Women Faculty in Science at the MIT, *The Massachusetts Institute of Technology Faculty Newsletter,* 11, (1999), 4.

90. Wimbauer, C., *Organisation, Geschlecht, Karriere. Fallstudien aus einem Forschungsinstitut.* Opladen, Leske und Budrich, 1999. **And**: Dekker, R., *De wetenschappelijke match. Persoon-cultuur fit en loopbanen van vrouwelijke en mannelijke wetenschappers.* Utrecht, 2000.

91. Balen, B. van, *Vrouwen in de wetenschappelijke arena: sociale uitsluiting in de universiteit,* Amsterdam, 2001. **And**: Bagilhole, B., & J. Goode, (2001), *op. cit.* **And**: Schiebinger, L., *Has Feminism changed Science?,* Cambridge, Harvard University Press, 1999.

92. Massachusetts Institute of Technology (MIT), (1999), *op.cit.*

93. Organisatie voor Strategisch Arbeidsmarktonderzoek, *Trendrapport Aanbod van arbeid 1999,* p. 9-12. **And**: Bekkering, J.M. & R.M.A. Jansweijer, *De verdeling van arbeid en zorg: prikkels en belemmeringen. Werkdocument van de Wetenschappelijke Raad voor het Regeringsbeleid,* Den Haag, 1998.

94. McCracken, D. M., (2000), *op.cit.,* p.166-167.

95. These phases and the checklist is largely derived from: Council of Europe, (1998), *op. cit..*

96. Verhaar, O., *Prima inter pares: over de voorkeursbehandeling van vrouwen: analyse van de argumantatiestrategieën van voor- en tegenstanders in de openbare discussie over het voorkeursbeleid.* Den Haag, Ministerie van Sociale Zaken en Werkgelegenheid, 1991.

97. Actually, a better translation would be "Gender Impact Assessment": the tool doesn't pursue a one-dimensional equal treatment between women and men, but explicitly takes into account the multi-layered working of gender mechanisms. We chose to use the term EER, though, to be able to distinguish this tool as a specific instrument in the 'general' category of gender impact assessments.

98. Verloo, M., & C. Roggenband, *Emancipatie-effect rapportage, theoretisch kader, methodiek en voorbeeldrapportages.* Den Haag, Ministerie van Sociale Zaken en Werkgelegenheid, 1994.

99. Graaf, H. van de, M. Mossink & J. Göflin, *Van de EER geleerd: een evaluatie van de emancipatie-effectrapportage.* Ministerie van Sociale Zaken en Werkgelgenheid, Directie Coordinatie Emancipatiebeleid, Nr. 110, januari 1999.

100. *Verloo, M., Making women count in the Netherlands. In: Beveridge, F., Nott, S. & K. Stephen (eds.), Making women count. Integrating gender into law and policymaking.* Ashgate, Aldershot, 2000, p.49-77. **And**: Plantenga, J., *Gender impact assessment and the employment strategy: the case of the Netherlands, external report for the European Commission.* October 2000. **And**: Verloo, M., & C. Roggenband, Gender Impact Assessment: the development of a New Instrument in the Netherlands. *Impact Assessment,* 14, (March 1996), 1, p.3-20.

101. These entrances for analysis are based on: Schiebinger, L., Creating

sustainable science. *Osiris,* 12, (1997), p.201-216.

102. Equal Opportunities Commission (EOC), A Checklist for Gender Proofing Research, Manchester, Cardiff, Glasgow, EOC, 2000.

103. The organistation recently changed its name into Organisatie voor Vrouwen in Hoger technisch Onderwijs en Posities (Organisation for Women in Higher technical Education and Positions) but decided to keep the familiar abbreviation of its old name VHTO.

104. These can be ordered at www.vhto.nl where you can also find more information about the project, in Dutch and English.

105. WiTEC, is a European database with information about women experts in Science, Engineering & Technology (SET) of 12 Member States.

106. Fischer, A., Rodriguez Mosquera, P.M., & K. Rojahn, *Masculiniteit met een feminien gezicht. Onderzoek naar de rol van organisatiecultuur in de trage doorstroming van vrouwen naar managementfuncties. Onderzoek in opdracht van het Ministerie van Sociale Zaken en Werkgelegenheid,* Den Haag, 2000.

107. Fischer, A., Rodriguez Mosquera, P.M., & K. Rojahn, (2000), *op.cit.*

108. Balen, B. van, *op. cit.* **And**: Bagilhole, B., & J. Goode, (2001), *op. cit.*

109. Portegijs, W. & M. Brugman, (1998), *op. cit.*

110. Portegijs, W., (1993), *op. cit.*

111. Chemers, M.M., *An Integrative Theory of Leadership,*1997. **And**: Fischer, (1998), *op. cit.* **And**: Jong, A.M., de & A. van Doorne-Huiskes, Leiderschapsstijlen, verschillen tussen mannen en vrouwen? In: Demenint, M.I. & C.E. Disselen (ed.), *Vrouwen, leiderschap en management.* Utrecht, 1992.

112. Brouns, M. & J. Sibbes, *Beeldvorming in taal en bedrijf. Een programma voor onderzoek naar sekse en organisatiecultuur.* Groningen, 1999. **And**: The Women Faculty Network, Massachusetts Institute of Technology (MIT), *Information Brochure for Incoming Women Faculty.* The Women Faculty Network, June 1992.

113. Brouns, M. & J. Sibbes, op.cit., 1999. **And**: Portegijs, W. & M. Brugman, (1998), *op.cit.* **And**: Collings, J. *Disciplining Academia: Women Academics and Possibilities for change. Women, Communication and power. Women in Leadership.* National Conference Papers, Edith Cowan University, 1992.

114. Mills, A.J., & P. Tancred, *Gendering Organisational Analysis.* Newbury Park, CA, Sage, 1992. **And**: Morgan, G., *Images of Organisation.* London, Sage, 1986. **And**: Wilson, F.M., Organisational behaviour and Gender, London, 1995. **And**: Fischer, A., (1999), *op. cit.*

115. Balen, B. van, *op.cit.,* 2001. **And**: Dekker, R., (2000), *op.cit.*

116. Scott, W.R., *Organisations: rational, national and open systems.* Englewood Cliffs, N.J., 1992. **And**: Mills, A.J., & P. Tancred, *op.cit.,* 1992.

117. Schiebinger, L., (1999), *op.cit.,* p.52.

118. Verbiest, (1999), *op. cit.* **And**: Tannen, D., *Gender and Discourse,* New York, Oxford, Oxford University Press, 1994.

119. Smelik, A., *Beelden van vrouwen, mannen en wetenschap. Een onderzoek naar beeldvorming en sekse aan de Universiteit van Maastricht,* Maastricht, 1998.

120. Meyerson, D.E., and J.K. Fletcher, (2000), *op. cit.*

Chapter III: Gender mainstreaming at universities: The process model approach

121. EFQM stands for European Foundation for Quality Management (EFQM). See more at: http://www.efqm.org
122. European Foundation for Quality Management (EFQM), Le Modèle EFQM d'Excellence, Brussel, 1999.
123. EFQM, (1999), *op. cit.*
124. Directie Gelijke Kansen, Federaal Ministerie van Tewerkstelling en Arbeid (MTA), *Integrating Equality into Total Quality Management according to the EFQM-model*, Brussel, 1999. **And:** Rijmenams, C. & E. Van Roy, Best Practices on Gender Mainstreaming in Belgium. Synthese, Brussel, Federaal Ministerie van Tewerkstelling en Arbeid (MTA), K.U.Leuven, 2000.
125. Directie Gelijke Kansen, MTA, (1999), *op.cit.*
126. Since April 1999 the Affirmative Action Unit is called Employment-Enterprises Unit and has become part of the Equal Opportunities Department of the Federal Ministry of Employment and Labour.
127. The project 'Putting the E into Quality' was a European collaboration between the 'Employment-Enterprises Unit' of the Equal Opportunities Department – Belgian Federal Ministry of Employment and Labour, and the following quality management centres: VCK (Vlaams Centrum voor Kwaliteitszorg), AWQ (Association Wallone pour la Gestion de la Qualité), IQA (Irish Quality Association).
128. Cel Positieve Acties, MTA, *Gelijke Kansen in Kwaliteitsgerichte Ondernemingen. Handleiding voor een Gelijke-Kansenbeleid, met voorbeelden en praktijkgetuigenissen*, *DRAFT 15/6/98*, Federaal Ministerie van Tewerkstelling en Arbeid (MTA) & Vlaams Centrum voor Kwaliteitszorg (VKZ), 1998.
129. Vlaams Centrum voor kwaliteitszorg (VCK), *Het EFQM excellentie Model*, *CD-ROM*. VCK, Zellik, 1999.
130. Dierickx, A., & E. Van Roy, *Equality Audit*, Ministerie van Tewerkstelling en Arbeid (MTA), Cel Positieve Acties, Brussel, 1997. **And:** Dierickx, A., & E. Van Roy, *Equality Checklist*, Ministerie van Tewerkstelling en Arbeid, Directie Gelijke Kansen, Brussel, 2000.
131. Nelen S., (2000), *op. cit.*
132. For instance: the ISI Science Citation Index.
133. For Flemish Universities see: Ministerie van de Vlaamse Gemeenschap, Departement Onderwijs, Administratie Hoger Onderwijs en Wetenschappelijk Onderzoek, *Aandacht voor kwaliteit in de Vlaamse universiteiten. Verslag van de Auditcommissie Kwaliteitszorg in het Academisch Onderwijs in Vlaanderen*. Brussel, 1998.
134. Belgian Association for Total Quality Management (BTQM), *Le Nouveau Modèle EFQM d'Excellence 1999*, Overijse, 23 november 2000.
135. This distinction between *by, for,* and *about* is based on the Women and Science initiative of the European Commission (see Chapter One).
136. Management Services, *Aanbod scholing en begeleiding*. Katholieke Universiteit

Nijmegen, Sector Personeel / Personeelsontwikkeling, 2000.

137. Lamoen, I. van & N. Leufkens, *Exit of interne ontwikkeling? Mobiliteit onder HBO-managers. Onderzoeksrapport in het kader van het project 'In&Uit-deel2'.* Nijmegen, Landelijk Steunpunt Emancipatie hbo (LSE), 2000. Available at http://www.Ise.han.nl

138. *NWO stands for Nederlandse Organisatie voor Wetenschappelijk Onderzoek. Translated: The Dutch Organisation for Scienctific Research.*

139. Bosch, M. & M. Potting, *Vrouwen moeten door dat plafond heen. Evaluatie van het Aspasia-programma, 1ᵉ ronde: ervaringen, resultaten, effecten.* Maastricht, 2001.

140. Frances Conley, quoted in: Schiebinger, L., (1999), op. cit., p.52.

141. Commission of the European Communities, COM (2000) 612, *op. cit.*

142. *Ibidem.*

143. These options are largely derived from: Vucht Tijssen, B.E. van, (2000), *op. cit.*

144. European Commission, *Fourth Framework Research Programme (1994-1998).* See http://europa.eu.int/comm/research/specpr.html

145. Seminar on a European Research Area. *Parallel Session on Valorising Human Resources*, Brussels, CCAB, 3 May 2000.

146. Marie Curie Training Grant Information Package, 1997, p.6, quoted from: Ackers L., (Project Director) et al., *The participation of women researchers in the TMR Marie Curie Fellowship.* 2000, p.7.

147. 'Doctoral' researchers are also called 'post-graduate' researchers.

148. Ackers L., (Project Director) et al., (2000), *op. cit.*, p.7.

149. *Ibidem.*

150. Ducatel, K., & J.C. Burgelman, *The Futures Project. Employment Map.* Joint Research Centre, European Commission, EUR19033EN, no. 13, 1999.

151. Vucht Tijssen, E.B., (2000), *op.cit.* **And**: Portegijs, W., (1998), *op.cit.*

152. Quoted from: Krummacher, S., *Equal Opportunities: a Necessity for quality in Research.* Contribution to Nature debate Why are there so Few Women in Science? 9 September 1999 - 14 October 1999. See: www.nature.com/ nature/debates/women/ women_navbar.html

153. European Commission (Osborn, M., Rees, T., Bosch, M. et al.), (2000), *op.cit.*, p.1.

154. Balen, B. van, (2001), *op.cit.*

155. Literally translated: 'Research Workshop'.

156. Quoted from: Bosch, M. (red.), I. Hoving & G. Wekker, (1999), *op. cit.*

157. *Ibidem.*

158. Gibbons, M. et al., *The new production of knowledge: the dynamics od science and research in contemporary societies*, London, Sage, 1994.

159. Berkhout, G.J., *The dynamic role of knowledge in innovation. A system of cyclic networks for the assessment of technological change and economic growth.* Delft University of Technology, 1999.

160. Lykke, N., *Women in Science: Sweden versus Denmark. A case Story about Neighbouring Countries whith Different Gender Profiles. Lecture for symposium Women*

and Science: The Dutch Case, organised by the Nederlands Genootschap Vrouwenstudies (NGV) on the occasion of the 73rd Lustrum of the Universiteit Utrecht, Utrecht, 17-04-2001.

161. This stands for 'Wet Evenredige Vertegenwoordiging van vrouwen in hogere functies in het hoger onderwijs'; which means: 'Law for Equal Representation of Women in senior functions in higher education'.

162. The full name of this law is: 'Modernisering Universitaire Bestuursstructuren', translated: 'Modernising University Governing Structures'.

163. Bosch, M., Discussiedossier emancipatiebeleid: naar een deltaplan voor total e-quality en diversiteit in de universiteit? *Tijdschrift voor Genderstudies*, jrg.1, nr. 4, (1998), p.46-54.

164. *Translation: Complaints Department*

165. Centrum voor Gelijke Kansenbeleid K.U.Leuven, Gelijke Kansenbeleid en Universiteit. Naar een Mainstreaming-benadering. Eerste Gelijke-Kansenrapport K.U.Leuven, Leuven, Centrum voor Gelijke Kansenbeleid, Oktober 1999, p.15-21.

166. The Mellow Good Practice Handbook, 1998 is available in Dutch, German and English and can be ordered at the following internet address http://www.vhto.nl.

167. Organisatie voor Strategisch Arbeidsmarktonderzoek, (1999), op. cit.p.9-12. **And**: Bekkering, J.M. & R.M.A. Jansweijer, (1998), *op. cit.*

168. Schneider Ross, Consultants in Diversity & Equality, Equality in the university – setting a New agenda. A Report on the Equality Audit for Cambridge University, Andover, Manor Courtyard Offices, January 2001.

169. Equality in the University. Introduction of the Vice-Chancellor. See: http://www. admin.cam.ac.uk/offices/personnel/equality/intro.html

170. Wennerås, C. & A. Wold, (1997), op.cit.

171. Brouns, M., (1999), op. cit.**And**: Abbot, A., Equality not taken for granted. *Nature*, vol.390, (1997) p.204. **And**: Grant, J., Burden, S. & G. Breen, No evidence of sexism in peer-review. *Nature*, Vol. 390, (1997), p.438. **And**: Wellcome Trust for Policy Research in Science and Medicine, *Women and Peer Review: An Audit of the Wellcome Trust's Decision-making on Grants.* London, Wellcome Trust for Policy Research in Science and Medicine, 1997.

172. European Commission (Osborn, M., Rees T., Bosch, M. et al.), (2000), op.cit., p.33-34.

173. Ackers L., (Project Director) et al., (2000), *op. cit.*

174. Ackers L., (Project Director) et al., (2000), *op. cit.*, p.8-9.

175. Ackers L., (Project Director) et al., (2000), *op. cit.*, p.58-99.

176. Two works in which the impact of such one-dimensional notions of quality are more extensively discussed are: Adviesraad voor het Wetenschaps- en Technologiebeleid (AWT), (2000), *op. cit.* **And**: Brouns, M., & H. Harbers, Kwaliteit in meervoud: reflectie op kwaliteiten van vrouwenstudies in Nederland. Den Haag, VUGA, 1994.

REFERENCES

Abbot, A., Equality not taken for granted. *Nature*, vol.390, (1997) p.204.

Ackers, L. (Project Director) et al., *The participation of women researchers in the TMR Marie Curie Fellowship*. 2000.

Adviesraad voor het Wetenschaps- en Technologiebeleid (AWT), *Halfslachtige Wetenschap. Onderbenutting van vrouwelijk potentieel als existentieel probleem voor academia*, AWT-Advies Nr. 43, Den Haag, AWT, 2000.

Area Development Management (ADM), *A manual for gender mainstreaming the local development social inclusion programme 2000-2006*. Dublin, November 2000.

Bagilhole, B., & J. Goode, The Contradiction of the Myth of Merit, and the Reality of a Patriarchal Support System in Academic Careers. A Feminist investigation. *The European Journal of Women's Studies*. 8, (2001), 2, p. 161-180.

Bagilhole, B., *Equal Opportunities and Social Policy*. Longman, 1997.

Bagilhole, B., How to keep a good woman down: an investigation of the role of institutional factors in the process of discrimination against women academics. In: *British Journal of Sociology of Education*,3 (14), (1999), p. 261-274.

Bagilhole, B., Survivors in a male preserve: a study of British women academics' experiences and perceptions of dicrimination in a UK University. In: *Higher Education*, 26 (1993), p.431-447.

Balen, B. van, & A. Fischer, *De universiteit als modern mannenklooster*, Amsterdam, 1998.

Balen, B. van, *Vrouwen in de wetenschappelijke arena: sociale uitsluiting in de universiteit*, Amsterdam, 2001.

Beckhoven, A. van, *Handleiding mainstreaming*. Den Haag, Ministerie van Sociale zaken en werkgelegenheid, Directie Coördinatie Emancipatiebeleid, 2000.

Bekkering, J.M. & R.M.A. Jansweijer, *De verdeling van arbeid en zorg: prikkels en belemmeringen. Werkdocument van de Wetenschappelijke Raad voor het Regerings-beleid*, Den Haag, 1998.

Belgian Association for Total Quality Management (BTQM), *Le Nouveau Modèle EFQM d'Excellence 1999*, Overijse, 23 november 2000.

Benschop, Y., & M. Verloo, Geen roos zonder doornen. Reflecties op main-streaming. In: *Tijdschrift voor Genderstudies*, 3 (4) (2001), p. 23-33.

Benschop, Y., & M. Verloo, *Gender in Balans. Mainstreaming gender in personeels-management, In opdracht van en in samenwerking met de dienst Emancipatiezaken van het Ministerie van de Vlaamse Gemeenschap*. Brussel, 1999.

Berkhout, G.J., *The dynamic role of knowledge in innovation. A system of cyclic networks for the assessment of technological change and economic growth*. Delft University of

Technology, 1999.

Bett, Sir M., *Independent review of Higher Education pay and conditions: Report of a Commitee chaired by Sir Michael Bett CBE*, London, The Stationary Office, 1999.

Blake, M., & I. La Valle, National Centre for Social Research, *Who applies for research funding? Key factors shaping funding application behaviour among women and men in British higher education institutions.*The Wellcome Trust, 2000.

Bosch, M. & M. Potting, *Vrouwen moeten door dat plafond heen. Evaluatie van het Aspasia-programma, 1ᵉ ronde: ervaringen, resultaten, effecten.* Maastricht, 2001.

Bosch, M. (red.), I. Hoving & G. Wekker, *In het hart van de wetenschap. Naar total E-quality en diversiteit in de universiteit.*AWT-Achtergrondstudie Nr. 15, Den Haag, Sdu Uitgevers, 1999.

Bosch, M., Discussiedossier emancipatiebeleid: naar een deltaplan voor total e-quality en diversiteit in de universiteit? *Tijdschrift voor Genderstudies*, jrg.1, nr. 4, (1998), p.46-54.

Bosch, M., Tussen bureaucratie en wetenschap. Twintig jaar universitaire emancipatie in Nederland. In: *Lover, Tijdschrift over feminisme, cultuur en wetenschap*, 99 (1999) 3.

Braithwaite, M., *Manual for integrating gender equality into local and regional development.* Brussels, Engender, 1998.

Brems, E., *Human Rights: Universality and Diversity*, Leuven, 1999.

Brouns, M. & J. Sibbes, *Beeldvorming in taal en bedrijf. Een programma voor onderzoek naar sekse en organisatiecultuur.* Groningen, 1999.

Brouns, M., & H. Harbers, *Kwaliteit in meervoud: reflectie op kwaliteiten van vrouwenstudies in Nederland.* Den Haag, VUGA, 1994.

Brouns, M., *De kwaliteit van het oordeel. Een onderzoek naar sekse en beoordelingssystemen van NWO en KNAW.* Utrecht, Nederlands Genootschap Vrouwenstudies, 1999.

Brouns, M., M. Verloo & M. Grünell (red.), *Vrouwenstudies in de jaren negentig. Een kennismaking vanuit verschillende disciplines.* Bussum, 1995.

Buikema, R., Meijer, M. & A. Smelik, Postmoderne cultuur en representatie. In: Brouns, M., Verloo, M. & M. Grünell (red.), *Vrouwenstudies in de jaren negentig. Een kennismaking vanuit verschillende disciplines.* Bussum, 1995, p.79-108.

Cameron, D., *Feminism and Linguistic theory.* London, MacMillan, 1992.

Caplan, P., *Lifting a ton of feathers: a woman's guide to surviving in the academic world.* Toronto, University of Toronto Press, 1993.

Cel Positieve Acties, MTA, *Gelijke Kansen in Kwaliteitsgerichte Ondernemingen. Handleiding voor een Gelijke-Kansenbeleid, met voorbeelden en praktijkgetuigenissen, DRAFT 15/6/98*, Federaal Ministerie van Tewerkstelling en Arbeid (MTA) & Vlaams Centrum voor Kwaliteitszorg (VKZ), 1998.

Centrum voor Gelijke Kansenbeleid K.U.Leuven, *Gelijke Kansenbeleid en Universiteit. Naar een Mainstreaming-benadering. Eerste Gelijke-Kansenrapport K.U.Leuven*, Leuven, Centrum voor Gelijke Kansenbeleid, Oktober 1999.

Centrum voor Gelijke Kansenbeleid K.U.Leuven, *Vooronderzoek. Gelijke Kansen bij aanstelling, benoeming en bevordering van het Zelfstandig Academisch Personeel aan de K.U.Leuven*, Leuven, Centrum voor Gelijke Kansenbeleid, Juni 2000.

Chemers, M.M., *An Integrative Theory of Leadership*,1997.

Collings, J., *Disciplining Academia: Women Academics and Possibilities for change. Women, Communication and power. Women in Leadership*. National Conference Papers, Edith Cowan University, 1992.

Collinson, D.L. & J. Hearn (eds.), *Men as managers, Managers as Men*. London – New York, Sage, 1996.

Commission of the European Communities, *Making a Reality of the European Research Area: Guidelines for EU Research Activities (2002-2006)*. COM(2000) 612, Brussels 4-10-2000.

Commission of the European Communities, *Women and Science: the Gender Dimension as a Leverage for Reforming Science*. Brussels, Commission Staff Working Paper, 15-05-2001, SEC (2001) 771.

Commission of the European Communities, *Women in Science. Mobilising women to enrich European research*, COM(1999)FINAL, Communication from the Comission Luxembourg, Office for Official publications of the European Communities of the European Commission.

Council of Europe, *Gender Mainstreaming. Conceptual Framework, Methodology and Presentation of Good Practices*. Strasbourg, Council of Europe, May 1998.

Crum, M., & J. Bal, *Werk- en loopbaanpositie van postdocs*. Leiden, Research voor Beleid, 1998.

Dekker, R., *De wetenschappelijke match. Persoon-cultuur fit en loopbanen van vrouwelijke en mannelijke wetenschappers*. Utrecht, 2000.

Dierickx, A., & E. Van Roy, *Equality Audit*, Ministerie van Tewerkstelling en Arbeid (MTA), Cel Positieve Acties, Brussel, 1997.

Dierickx, A., & E. Van Roy, *Equality Checklist*, Ministerie van Tewerkstelling en Arbeid, Directie Gelijke Kansen, Brussel, 2000.

Directie Gelijke Kansen, Federaal Ministerie van Tewerkstelling en Arbeid (MTA), *Integrating Equality into Total Quality Management according to the EFQM-model*, Brussel, 1999.

Ducatel, K., & J.C. Burgelman, *The Futures Project. Employment Map*. Joint Research Centre, European Commission, EUR19033EN, no. 13, 1999.

Emmerick, H. van, Dekker, R., & Claringbould, I., Waarom gaat het zo langzaam? Enkele observaties vanuit de praktijk van het universitaire emancipatiebeleid. In: *Tijdschrift voor Genderstudies*, 3 (1) (2000), p. 49-58.

Equal Opportunities Commission (EOC), A Checklist for Gender Proofing Research, Manchester, Cardiff, Glasgow, EOC, 2000.

Equal Opportunities Commission (EOC), *A good practice guide. How to set targets for gender equality*. Manchester, Cardiff and Glasgow, EOC, January 2001.

Equal Pay Task Force, *Just Pay. A report to the Equal Opportunities Commission*. Manchester, Equal Opportunities Commission (EOC), 2001.

European Commission (Osborn, M., Rees T., Bosch, M. et al.), *Science Policies in the European Union. Promoting Excellence through Mainstreaming Gender Equality. A Report from the ETAN Expert Group on Women and Science*. Luxembourg, European Commission, Office for Official Publications of the European Communities, 2000.

European Commission, *Incorporating Equal Opportunities for Women and Men into All Community Policies and Activities*, Communication from the Commission, COM(96)97FINAL.

European Commission, *Women and Science: Networking the Networks. Declaration of Networks Active in Europe*, Brussels, July 8&9, 1999.

European Foundation for Quality Management (EFQM), Le Modèle EFQM d'Excellence, Brussel, 1999.

Federaal Ministerie van Tewerkstelling en Arbeid (MTA), Directie Gelijke Kansen, *Mainstreaming in het federaal tewerkstellingsbeleid. Evaluatie en statistische hinderpalen*. Brussels, MTA, december 2000.

Fischer, A., *De top (m/v): de paradox van emoties*. Amsterdam, 1998.

Fischer, A., *Normen, waarden en gedrag in de organisatie. In opdracht van het Ministerie van Landbouw, Natuurbeheer en Visserij*. Den Haag, 1999.

Fischer, A., Rodriguez Mosquera, P.M., & K. Rojahn, *Masculiniteit met een feminien gezicht. Onderzoek naar de rol van organisatiecultuur in de trage doorstroming van vrouwen naar managementfuncties. Onderzoek in opdracht van het Ministerie van Sociale Zaken en Werkgelegenheid*, Den Haag, 2000.

Fitzgerald, R., *Toolkit for Mainstreaming Equal Opportunities in the European Structural Funds. A practical Guide to plan Preparation and Implementation*. Glasgow, Equal Opportunities Commission (EOC) & HERA 2001, 2000.

Flynn, G., Deloitte & Touche changes women's minds. *Personnel Journal, 75*, (April 1996), 4, p.56-68.

Fogelberg, P. (ed.) et al., *Hard work at the Academy: Research and Interventions on Gender Inequalities in Higher Education*. Helsinki, Helsinki University press, 1999.

Fruytier, B. & V. Timmerhuis, *Mensen in Onderzoek. Het mobiliseren van HRM in wetenschapsorganisaties*. Assen, Van Gorcum, 1995.

Georgi, H., Is there an unconscious discrimination against women in science? *APS News*, (2000), p.8.

Gibbons, M. et al., *The new production of knowledge: the dynamics od science and research in contemporary societies*, London, Sage, 1994.

Glover, J. & J. Fielding, Women in the sciences in britain: getting in? In: *Journal of Education and Work*, 1 (12), (1999), p. 57-73.

Goode, J. & B. Bagilhole, Gendering the management of change in Higher Education: a Case Study. In: *Gender, Work and Organisation*, 3 (5), (1998), p. 148-164.

Goode, J., & B. Bagilhole, A social construction of gendered equal opportunities in UK Universities: a case study of women technicians. In: *Critical Social Policy*, 2 (18), (1998), p.175-192.

Graaf, H. van de, M. Mossink & J. Göflin, *Van de EER geleerd: een evaluatie van de emancipatie-effectrapportage*. Ministerie van Sociale Zaken en Werkgelgenheid, Directie Coordinatie Emancipatiebeleid, Nr. 110, januari 1999.

Grant, J., Burden, S. & G. Breen, No evidence of sexism in peer-review. *Nature*, Vol. 390, (1997), p.438.

Hoogland, R.C.& Steen, M. v. d., *Gender and/in European Research: The Fifth Frame-*

work Programme of the European Community for Research, Technological Development and Demonstration Activities (1998-2002), Amsterdam.

International Labour Office (ILO), *Guidelines for the Integration of Gender Issues into the Design, Monitoring and Evaluation of ILO Programmes and Projects.*

Jong, A.M., de & A. van Doorne-Huiskes, Leiderschapsstijlen, verschillen tussen mannen en vrouwen? In: Demenint, M.I. & C.E. Disselen (ed.), *Vrouwen, leiderschap en management.* Utrecht, 1992.

Keijzer, B.S.C. & E.H. Gordijn, *Resultaten arbeidsmarktenquête jonge wetenschappers.* Ondernemingsraad Projectmedewerkers NWO en landelijk AIO en OIO Overleg, 2000.

Keuzenkamp, S., Van vrouwenstudies naar emancipatiebeleid. In: *Tijdschrift voor Genderstudies,* 2 (3) (1999), p. 43-53.

Krummacher, S., *Equal Opportunities: a Necessity for quality in Research.* Contribution to Nature debate Why are there so Few Women in Science? 9 September 1999 - 14 October 1999.

Lamoen, I. van & N. Leufkens, *Exit of interne ontwikkeling? Mobiliteit onder HBO-managers. Onderzoeksrapport in het kader van het project 'In&Uit-deel2'.* Nijmegen, Landelijk Steunpunt Emancipatie hbo (LSE), 2000. Available at http://www.Ise.han.nl

Lamoen, I. van, & N. Leufkens, *Een andere kijk op de WEV: Female resources management in het HBO. Onderzoeksrapport in het kader van het project In & Uit – Deel I.* Nijmegen, Landelijk Steunpunt Emancipatie HBO (LSE), 2000.

Lamoen, I. van, *Gender mainstreaming: een goed begin is het halve werk. Een inventarisatie en evaluatie van het emancipatiebeleid aan Nederlandse universiteiten. In opdracht van de Katholieke Universiteit Leuven.* Nijmegen, 1999.

Lykke, N., *Women in Science: Sweden versus Denmark. A case Story about Neighbouring Countries whith Different Gender Profiles. Lecture for symposium Women and Science: The Dutch Case,* organised by the Nederlands Genootschap Vrouwenstudies (NGV) on the occasion of the 73rd Lustrum of the Universiteit Utrecht, Utrecht, 17-04-2001.

Management Services, *Aanbod scholing en begeleiding.* Katholieke Universiteit Nijmegen, Sector Personeel / Personeelsontwikkeling, 2000.

Massachusetts Institute of Technology (MIT), A Study on the Status of Women Faculty in Science at the MIT, *The Massachusetts Institute of Technology Faculty Newsletter,* 11, (1999), 4.

McCracken, D. M., Winning the talent war for women: sometimes it takes a revolution. *Harvard Business Review,* 78, (November-December 2000), 6, p.159-167.

McNeil, L. & M. Sher, *Dual-Science-Career Couples: Survey results,* North Carolina, Virginia, 1998

Meyerson, D.E. & J.K. Fletcher, A Modest Manifesto for Shattering the Glass Ceiling, *Harvard Business Review,* (January-February 2000).

Mills, A.J., & P. Tancred, *Gendering Organisational Analysis.* Newbury Park, CA, Sage, 1992.

Ministerie van de Vlaamse Gemeenschap, Departement Onderwijs, Administratie Hoger Onderwijs en Wetenschappelijk Onderzoek, *Aandacht voor kwaliteit in de Vlaamse universitieten. Verslag van de Auditcommissie Kwaliteitszorg in het Academisch Onderwijs in Vlaanderen.* Brussel, 1998.

Morgan, G., *Images of Organisation.* London, Sage, 1986.

Morley, L. & N. Rassool, *School Effectiveness: Fracturing the Discourse.* London, Falmer Press, 1999.

Nelen, S., Mainstreaming als 'nieuwe' strategie inzake gelijke-kansenbeleid: wondermiddel of verdwijntruc? *Tijdschrift voor Genderstudies,* 3/4, (2000), p.33-42.

Noordenbos, G., Genderassymetrie in de aanvraag van onderzoekssubsidies. *Tijdschrift voor Genderstudies,* 2/4, (1999), p.36-45.

O'Leary, V.E. & J.M. Mitcell, Women connecting with Women: Networks and Mentors in the United States. In: Lie, S.S. & V.E. O'Leary (eds.), *Storming the Tower. Women in the academic World.* London, Kogan Page, 1990.

Organisatie voor Strategisch Arbeidsmarktonderzoek, *Trendrapport Aanbod van arbeid 1999.*

Pearson W. Jr., & I. Fechter (eds.), *Who will do science? Educating the next generation.*Baltimore, John Hopkins University Press, 1994.

Plantenga, J., *Gender impact assessment and the employment strategy: the case of the Netherlands, external report for the European Commission.* October 2000.

Portegijs, W., & M. Brugman, *Eerdaags Evenredig? Belemmeringen en beleid ten aanzien van de doorstroom van vrouwen naar hogere wetenschappelijke functies.* Beleidsgerichte Studies Hoger Onderwijs en Wetenschapsbeleid, Den Haag, 1998.

Portegijs, W., *Jammer dat u gaat: het snelle verloop van vrouwelijke wetenschappers: een lek in het emancipatiebeleid.* Utrecht, 1993.

Rees, T., Gender Mainstreaming. In: Watson, S., & L. Doyal, (eds.), *Engendering Social Policy,* Milton Keynes, Open University Press, 1998:1, p. 165-183.

Rees, T., *Mainstreaming Equality in the European Union.* London, Routledge, 1998.

Rees, T., *Women and the EC Training Programmes: Tinkering, Tailoring, Transforming.* Bristol, University of Bristol, SAUS Publications, 1995.

Rijmenams, C. & E. Van Roy, *Best Practices on Gender Mainstreaming in Belgium. Synthese.* Brussel, Federaal Ministerie van Tewerkstelling en Arbeid (MTA), K.U.Leuven, 2000.

Schiebinger, L., Creating sustainable science. *Osiris,* 12, (1997), p.201-216.

Schiebinger, L., *Has Feminism changed Science?,* Cambridge, Harvard University Press, 1999.

Schneider Ross, Consultants in Diversity & Equality, *Equality in the university – setting a New agenda. A Report on the Equality Audit for Cambridge University,* Andover, Manor Courtyard Offices, January 2001.

Scott, W.R., *Organisations: rational, national and open systems.* Englewood Cliffs, N.J., 1992.

Seminar on a European Research Area. *Parallel Session on Valorising Human Resources,* Brussels, CCAB, 3 May 2000.

Smelik, A., *Beelden van vrouwen, mannen en wetenschap. Een onderzoek naar beeldvor-

ming en sekse aan de Universiteit van Maastricht, Maastricht, 1998.

Swiebel, J., Mainstreaming als verdwijntruc. In: *Lover*, 2 (1999), p.4-8.

Tannen, D., *Gender and Discourse*, New York, Oxford, Oxford University Press, 1994.

The Wellcome Trust for Policy Research in Science and Medicine, *Women and Peer Review: An Audit of the Wellcome Trust's Decision-making on Grants*. London, The Wellcome Trust for Policy Research in Science and Medicine, 1997.

The Women Faculty Network, Massachusetts Institute of Technology (MIT), *Information Brochure for Incoming Women Faculty*. The Women Faculty Network, June 1992.

Thomas, K., *Gender and Subject in Higher Education*. Milton Keynes, Open University Press, 1990.

Universiteit Utrecht, Bestuurscommissie Emancipatiebeleid, *Vooruit v/m*, Utrecht, 1998.

Valian, V. *Why so Slow? The Advancement of Women. Carrier Patterns of Women Academics are Slow due to Lack of Support and Inadequate Information*. Cambridge, Massachusetts, MIT Press, 1999.

Van Nuland, Y. et al., *Doorbraak door uitmuntendheid. Het EFQM-model duidelijk voor iedereen*. Blanden, Comatech, 1997.

Verbiest, A., *Zaken zijn zaken. Taal en de kwaliteit van beleid*. Den Haag, Ministerie van Sociale Zaken en Werkgelegenheid, 1999.

Verhaar, O., *Prima inter pares: over de voorkeursbehandeling van vrouwen: analyse van de argumantatiestrategieën van voor- en tegenstanders in de openbare discussie over het voorkeursbeleid*. Den Haag, Ministerie van Sociale Zaken en Werkgelegenheid, 1991.

Verloo, M., & C. Roggenband, *Emancipatie-effect rapportage, theoretisch kader, methodiek en voorbeeldrapportages*. Den Haag, Ministerie van Sociale Zaken en Werkgelegenheid, 1994.

Verloo, M., & C. Roggenband, Gender Impact Assessment: the development of a New Instrument in the Netherlands. *Impact Assessment*, 14, (March 1996), 1, p.3-20.

Verloo, M., Making women count in the Netherlands. In: Beveridge, F., Nott, S. & K. Stephen (eds.), *Making women count. Integrating gender into law and policymaking*. Ashgate, Aldershot, 2000, p.49-77.

Vlaams Centrum voor kwaliteitszorg (VCK), *Het EFQM excellentie Model, CD-ROM*. VCK, Zellik, 1999.

Vucht Tijssen, B.E. van, *Talent voor de Toekomst. Toekomst voor Talent. Plan van aanpak voor het wetenschapspersoneelsbeleid*. Utrecht, 2000.

Watson, S., & L. Doyal, (eds.), *Engendering Social Policy*, Milton Keynes, Open University Press, 1998.

Weert, E., de & B.E. Vucht Tijssen, van, Academic Staff between threat and opportunity: changing employment and conditions of service. In: Jongbloed, B., Maassen, P. & G. Neave (eds.), *From the eye of the storm. Higher education's changing institution*. Dordrecht, Kluwer, 1999, p. 39-65.

Wennerås, C. & A. Wold, Nepotism and Sexism in Peer Review. Commentary.

Nature, (1997), 22.

Wilson, F.M., Organisational behaviour and Gender, London, 1995.

Wimbauer, C., *organisation, Geschlecht, Karriere. Fallstudien aus einer Forschungs-institut.* Opladen, Leske und Budrich, 1999.

Wimbauer, C., *Organisation, Geschlecht, Karriere. Fallstudien aus einem Forschungs-institut.* Opladen, Leske und Budrich, 1999.

Zimmermann, K., *Spiele mit Macht in der Wissenschaft. Passfähigkeit und Geschlecht als Kriterien für Berufungen,* Berlin, Edition Sigma, 2000.